Solve My Mortgage Mess *Now!*

Solve My Mortgage Mess *Now!*

Facing Foreclosure?
Upside Down on Your Mortgage?

Solve Your Mortgage Mess NOW
with Strategies Revealed in this Practical
Step by Step Resource Guide
to Help You Get It Done!

**CHARLES W. CHRISTMAS, JR.,
ESQ., CMA, SMA**

For information visit: www.SolveMyMortgageMessNow.com

Printed in the United States of America

First Edition

For information about special discounts for bulk purchases contact www.SolveMyMortgageMessNow.com

ISBN 978-0-9833287-0-4
Published by PS11977GROUP, LLC

Dedication

Gratefully, I dedicate this book to the one who makes it possible for one to "owe no one anything but love." Additionally, this book is dedicated to my six children, whom I love, and to all the people who have supported me and believed in me over the years, showing me their love each in their own special and unique ways. Lastly, this book is dedicated to my colleagues and to the people I have been privileged to meet and come to know as they find their own way out of the mortgage mess.

Contents

Foreword

LIVING IN CLARK COUNTY, NEVADA, where Las Vegas, North Las Vegas, and Henderson are located, has certainly given me a first-hand look into the mortgage mess that has come upon our nation like a curse. In Clark County, approximately 600 homes are sold each day in foreclosure auctions. Over a five-day week that totals approximately 3,000 per week and almost 150,000 per year. If one calculates that on average there are 2.5 people living in each home then each year about 375,000 people are stressed out, run through the wringer, and put on the street. To add some perspective, that is roughly the same size as the entire population of Tampa, or Pittsburgh, or St Louis, or Miami, or Cincinnati. Imagine the entire population of any one of those cities stressed out, devastated, and on the street. So whatever else you may know or not know, you can know that you are not alone.

You may have picked up this book out of curiosity, but probably more out of a hope to find some answer or some solution to your own personal situation. Perhaps you are interested on behalf of someone near to you, like a family member or a close friend. Well, that is the purpose of this book: to not only give hope, but also to inform you of some concrete real-time, real-world strategies that will help you break out of this mortgage mess and regain your peace of mind and your economic foundation, the latter of which was almost taken for granted until a few short years ago. In this book you will learn many things that you had probably never expected you would need to know. Nonetheless, the information in this book is crucial if you are going to free yourself of the mortgage mess that is plaguing our nation and many individuals at this time. My hope is that you will be able to see the light at the end of the tunnel and actually exit the tunnel into the light of day with a bright future ahead of you. **NOTE:** It is important that you read this book in order, as it builds upon itself; this way you will better appreciate the subsequent information. For that reason, let's agree now that you will read this book in order. Agreed? Okay, great! Let's begin.

First Things First:

Seek the Advice of Your Own Attorney.
This Book Does Not Give Legal Advice.
Do Not Rely On This Book For Legal Advice.

Essential Disclaimer

Please read т*his important disclaimer for your benefit!* This book is not intended to, nor does it give any legal advice. There may be legal *information* found here, but you must not take it as *advice* for your situation. You must consult your own attorney with his or her opinion to decide if anything mentioned in this book is appropriate and suitable for you in your unique situation. This book is only one man's opinion, that of the author. Others may disagree and have opinions to the contrary. The purpose of this book is to help you think, but you must still consider the experienced and educated opinion of your own professional representative. This book is not intended to be a scholarly work with lots of citations for sources because that would take much longer to produce. Timeliness is important in getting this book out because every day that goes by more and more American family homes are stolen from their rightful owners. The ravages of foreclosure are being thrust upon the members of families who are without the knowledge of assistance that may available to them, as they are mired in the daily abuse of large, greedy corporations.

Limit of Liability and Disclaimer of Warranty

While the publisher and author have used their best efforts in preparing this book, they make no representations or warranties with respect to the accuracy or completeness of the contents of this book and specifically disclaim any implied warranties of merchantability or fitness for a particular purpose. No warranty may be created or extended by sales representatives or written sales materials. The techniques and strategies contained herein may not be suitable for your situation. You should consult with a professional, where appropriate. Neither the publisher nor the author shall be liable for any loss of profit or any other damages, commercial or otherwise, including but not limited to special, incidental, consequential, or other damages.

Introduction

THERE ARE FEW THINGS IN LIFE worse than being in a tough situation that is complicated with the dynamic of experiencing little or no control over the outcome. Most of us will accept difficulties that come our way as long as we are at least given a fighting chance to have some influence or impact upon the final result. This is especially true in situations where we are responsible for the well-being and welfare of others, such as a spouse or our children. When we are thrust into a difficult situation and not given a fighting chance then the difficulty is magnified. This, in turn, puts more pressure on the true treasures in life, such as relationships, self-image, confidence, rational thought, emotional well-being, and even physical health.

The mortgage mess in our nation has put many individuals in a personal situation exactly as has been described above. It is not fun. It is very painful, and it is very destructive in many ways both seen and unseen. Far too many citizens of our nation and our communities have been harassed and subjected to extreme difficulties through no fault of their own. So now it is time for a change. It is time for hope and a new awareness of the resources that can be used to bring an end to the seeming madness that is affecting our neighborhoods and causing so much upheaval and distress in far too many of our homes, lives, families, and communities.

The purpose of this book is to restore your vitality in life, and to stop the stress caused by the forces of corporate greed and arrogance. By first understanding the nature and the origin of a problem, it is possible to effectuate a solution to the problem. With that knowledge and understanding comes then the renewed hope and energy to do something about the problem. However, this particular problem, which has become known as the mortgage mess, was not created like just any other problem. It was very craftily designed, and it takes particular and special resources and assistance to stop it and find a workable exit from it.

So as the book proceeds, we will look at the current nature and effects of the problem, and what it is doing to many of us who are affected by it. Additionally, we will look at the causes of the problem to understand just how it came about. Further, we will examine some of the players and prime movers that performed various roles in the problem as it was created as well as those who continue to play active roles in it today. Best of all, we are going to review concrete real-world strategies to actually stop the mortgage mess as it tries to come against you or your loved ones. The help in this book will not only include special techniques and actions you can take by utilizing the laws of the land, but will also reveal states of mind and attitudes that will help you take advantage of contributions that will work to restore your sense of liberty and self-esteem. This book will instruct you on how to find the right resources to assist you, since you will rarely, if ever, be able to accomplish this completely on your own. That's okay. You didn't get into this situation by yourself, and you don't have to get out of it all by yourself either. Help is available. Lastly, this book will give you various resources to help you put together a plan to make your best and most appropriate breakout from this mortgage mess.

So take heart. Renew your hope. Take a deep breath. Regain your sense of humor, and get ready to find your own best exit out of this horrible situation we call "the mortgage mess." Better days are coming, and they are starting right now.

PART ONE

The Beginning

CHAPTER ONE

Pain(t)ing a Picture of the Problem

SEPTEMBER 11, 2001, WAS AN immeasurable shock to the American psyche in many ways. But as a resilient nation with a culture of strength, the American people bounced back, continued to work, and the economy seemed to take off and soar. Prosperity was in the air as many people started new businesses and corporate America logged record profits. Housing demand was strong and prices continued to rise year after year, especially in the developing locations of California, Arizona, Nevada, and Florida where sun belt demand was strong. Many other locations around the country also experienced robust business climates and surges in new home construction, as well as soaring home prices, in general. The dot.com bubble that had burst on Wall Street was only a faint memory by now. As a nation, America had overcome the dot.com bubble burst as well as a direct attack from enemies who invaded the homeland for the first time in modern history. All seemed to be well, but there was a terrible menace brewing beneath the surface that would not be noticed or seen for some time to come.

Many people who lived in California found that they could sell their property in California and buy a home twice the size in Nevada for half the selling price of their California home. That meant there was money left over for their choice of new property. This seemed to be such a perfect storm that many people starting moving or retiring to the greater Las Vegas area from not only California but other parts of the country as well. For many months approximately 7,000 people moved to Las Vegas each month. Approximately 30,000 to 35,000 new homes were constructed each year in Clark County, Nevada. Roads, parks, as many as thirteen new schools per year, shopping centers, and fire stations were all built at record pace as the economy cruised in sixth gear like a new high-performance Lamborghini or Ferrari sports car.

The typical home construction utilizes about twenty-two different trades, and also uses mortgage brokers, real estate agents, title companies, advertising agencies, moving companies, and interior decorators; in turn, new home sales increase furniture and appliance sales, insurance sales, and on and on. So the housing construction truly is the engine that pulls the American economy along to greater and greater heights of the American dream. However, the American dream is dependent upon certain core values and assumptions. If those prerequisites are not there, then it is possible for the American dream to become the American nightmare. Essentially, that is exactly what happened without really being noticed from approximately 2001 until 2007. It was a seven-year period that was thought to be one of the heights of prosperity in American history, but it has brought a death knell of economic disaster with a hangover worse than too much cheap screw-top wine bought on sale from a convenience store.

Mortgage money was very easy to come by, as there was little, if any, pre-qualification of the borrowers (in other words, to see if, in fact, they were going to be capable of repaying the loans that were so freely given to them). For instance, there was the "No Doc Loan." This simply meant that no documents, such as bank statements, employment records, pay stubs, tax returns, etc., were required to make the loan. Then there was the "Stated Income Loan" which meant, basically, that the borrower, or as was usually the case the borrower's mortgage representative, simply stated the income of the borrower on the mortgage application with no verification, and usually without the knowledge or consent of the borrower. Then there was the classic "NINJA Loan," which was a cute acronym for "no income, no job or assets." The long-used, tried-and-true standards for making mortgage loans were simply being relaxed and put aside so that more and more loans could be made, so more houses could be purchased, so more houses could be built, so the economy could support and create more jobs, and on and on. Some would say that the Republicans wanted more jobs and cheap labor, and the Democrats wanted more and more people to own houses. Either way, the result seems to be just two sides of the same coin in many cases. Whether Democrat or Republican, the same abuses occurred.

With so much money available, it was possible for many persons—for example, gambling dealers or catering employees at the large casinos in Las Vegas—to purchase as many as twenty properties over a period of a year or two. There were people who perhaps made a salary of $50,000 per year, but they owned and controlled and managed twenty rental properties worth collectively five to ten million dollars. That is almost incredible, but in actuality it was common. Making money was easy. There were as many as a hundred names on waiting lists to purchase properties in almost every subdivision development in Las Vegas. There were lotteries and drawings to see who would be fortunate enough to be selected to purchase a property. Meanwhile, most builders automatically raised their prices categorically every two weeks without fail. So if you were lucky enough to have your name selected, you could put the property under contract, and when it was finished five or six months later you could either flip it (sell it for a profit) or keep it and rent it out. As prices rose, "equity" was created, and the homes could be refinanced every year or so to pull out more cash for purchasing yet more houses, if one so chose. However, cash usually was not required because the homes could be 100 percent financed with an 80 percent first mortgage and a 20 percent second mortgage. No problem, just sign on the dotted lines. Who's next?

However, the chickens slowly began their U-turn in late 2006. Soon they would be in full flight looking for a place to roost. Prices weren't increasing quite as fast. What's more, prices were beginning to be stratospheric. People began to question if prices could truly continue to rise and rise forever. Goldman Sachs began to publicly question some of the values of its own investments that were based on the housing market; and slowly, at first, but surely at last the market began to creak, crack, and then croak. Many people were caught without warning and were blindsided. At first people thought to refinance, pull out cash to be able to hang on. But that was not going to work. Demand ground to a halt. Values began to tumble, and tumble they did. Values now in Clark County have fallen at least 60 percent and some say even more. Today many foreclosure properties sell at auction for only 25 to 30 percent of their value in 2006. Many properties that have been foreclosed upon are not even put on the market for fear of bringing the market down even further.

But what happened to the family that had moved to Las Vegas from California or somewhere simply looking to find a better job in a booming economy, buy a new house with easy money available, and had no idea of what was to come? How well did they fare? Let's look at a hypothetical couple, Bob and Mary Jones and their two children Jenny and Johnny. Perhaps Bob and Mary were not able to keep their jobs as the economy began to shrink, conventions were canceled, party goers coming to Vegas declined, home construction began to slow down, and all the supporting businesses began to have less and less work available, and less need for employees. Payments on the two new cars and the boat now seemed a burden and took the joy out of driving and sailing. Credit card advances helped make the payments for awhile; but eventually it became too much, and Bob and Mary had to let the boat go back to the dealer from which it had been purchased. The Harley they used to enjoy riding on road trips was now also gone, as the payments were too much to maintain. For awhile, Bob and Mary were able to keep the payments up on their mortgage. After all, that was the most valuable asset among all they owned, and it was also their *home*. The cruise they had booked had to be cancelled, and the deposit was lost. After some time, Bob had to ask Mary to give up the car that she loved because if they kept it they would not be able to make the mortgage payments. Jenny and Johnny began to notice that Mommy and Daddy did not seem to be as happy as they used to be. They noticed, too, that Mommy and Daddy were arguing much more often, and shouting at each other in a way they had never seen before.

Now Bob and Mary were down to one car. Mary was looking for any work she could find. However, it just seemed that no one was interested in hiring interior decorators at this time. Bob had been successful working as a mortgage representative, but now it seemed that no one wanted to finance a new purchase or refinance an existing property. Their $200,000-a-year income that afforded them a luxury lifestyle had simply vanished right before their eyes. Their house was truly beautiful, as it was a 3,600-square-foot home in a gated community with a tropical pool in the rear, and a three-car garage. Nonetheless, Bob and Mary could hardly appreciate the beauty because all they could think about was the $500,000 first mortgage, and the $150,000 second mortgage that had been used to install the pool and make down payments on the cars, the boat, and the motorcycle. The payments were easy enough at the beginning, when Bob and Mary were employed, but now they were impossible to make because both Bob and Mary were out of work, and the loan on the first mortgage had just adjusted, which increased the payment from $2,000 per month to $3,500 per month. On top of that was the second mortgage payment of $1,000 per month, the real estate taxes of $400 per month, and the homeowners' association dues of $100 per month. Bob had already used up his 401k savings trying to keep up with the payments. And Mary still had school loans she was paying to get her degree as an interior designer.

The worst part of it all was that their home, which had been worth close to a million dollars at the height of the housing market, was now worth only $275,000, yet their mortgage balance was almost $700,000 (the negative amortization from the first few years had been added to the outstanding principal amount).

The phone calls from the collection agencies were more than Mary could take. At first, she would answer their call and talk to them. Many times, Jenny and Johnny would see their mom cry after she hung up the phone. The people who made the calls seemed incapable of understanding; and many times, they were rude and pushy. Finally, in the end Mary and Bob just stopped answering the calls. Johnny and Jenny would be frightened if the phone rang and they went to answer it thinking it was one of their friends calling, only to hear Mommy and Daddy shout together, "Don't answer that phone!"

The children noticed strange people sitting in cars in front of their home taking photographs. Sometimes they would come to the door and ask if they could come inside and take pictures of the house. Bob and Mary instructed Jenny and Johnny not to answer the door unless one of the parents was there and said it was okay. The children noticed that their dad was smoking more, and also drinking more, and even drinking around the house in the daytime, which had never been their dad's custom before. They also noticed that their mom was spending more time with her friends and less and less time at home. Whenever the parents were together at home there was not much communication except for arguing about money, and all the mistakes that the other person had made in the past. The kids heard the parents begin to accuse each other more and more. The kids now were afraid and wanted to spend more time away from home with their own friends.

Finally, the day came and there was a notice taped on the front door of the house saying that the house was going to be sold in three weeks for lack of payments. Bob and Mary had simply run out of money, and had not made a payment in almost six months. They had tried the loan modification solution, but without any success. The only result they saw was that someone posing as a loan modification expert took $3,500 of their money and got no result. When they went back to try to get a refund, they found out that the business was no longer there; in fact, it had gone out of business.

Finally, Mary decided she could not take it all any longer, so she filed for a divorce from Bob. It is very easy and quick to get a divorce in Las Vegas. So even though the divorce was not finalized yet, all the family had to move out of their dream home into an apartment. However, there was one big problem. The apartment complex did not take pets. The Jones family had a Labrador retriever, a cat, and two birds. As they packed and pulled away from their home on that Saturday morning, Bob had left all the animals in the garage. He did leave some food and water, and he said that hopefully someone would find the pets and arrange homes for them. However, in his mind Bob wondered if that would really happen or not. Mainly, he said that to keep the children from crying too much. Bob himself was sad about leaving the pets, but he was so stressed out about everything that he couldn't think straight. Mary was going to eventually move in with her parents back in California, and take the children with her. Bob had not decided what exactly he was going to do. He knew he needed to find some kind of work somewhere before he could even think of anything. He was broke, busted, disgusted, and down and out big time. The children had always felt like Mommy and Daddy could protect them from the pressures of the outside world, but now Johnny and Jenny were no longer sure of much of anything. Their home was gone, their pets were gone, and even their family was soon to be gone. Now they had to move away from all their friends, and they had no idea what the future would be. All they knew was they were scared.

Bob and Mary's credit was ruined. Their finances were exhausted from trying to hold on to a house that was now worth less than half of the debt on it. Through it all, they had allowed the stress of everything to get between them and drive them apart. But the problem is not just with Bob and Mary. It is also a multi-generational problem because Johnny and Jenny will be affected for the rest of their lives by what has happened to them over the past year. It will be more difficult for them to trust anything or anyone. It will be difficult for them to make lasting commitments, not knowing whether the commitments will hold together or not. And as it turns out, the pets did not survive. The desert climate heat proved to be too much for all the pets. The stench was overwhelming when a home inspector for the lender finally showed up to check on the property.

This hypothetical story may sound too bizarre, but believe me it is only typical of so many people. Families, individuals, children, and pets by the thousands and scores of thousands have experienced almost precisely what has been portrayed in this brief depiction. You see, the mortgage mess is not just about money. It is about human lives and relationships. That is the deepest loss in it all. The scars run deep and the pain is all too real. The sleepless nights are too many, the divorces are far too many, the frightened children are exceedingly too many, and the suffering even of the pets are too numerous to log.

Now let's look briefly at the neighbors of the Joneses. Just down the street from the former home of the Jones family live Jose and Maria Gonzales and Paul and Gina Schwartz. We will first become acquainted with the Gonzales. The Gonzales have been married for ten years, have three children, and both still have good paying jobs, working as a dentist and a dental assistant in a local clinic. It seems that no matter what the economy, everyone still wants to take care of their teeth and stop the pain if there is a problem. So in some ways the Gonzales family was protected from the current recession, but there was still one glaring problem. The home of the Gonzales was very similar to that of Bob and Mary Jones. Unfortunately, their mortgage was also similar. That is, their first mortgage was almost $500,000, but like the Jones family, their home was now only worth about $275,000. The Gonzales were current with their monthly mortgage payments, but each month they kept looking for a solution and wondered how much longer they should pay on a mortgage that could almost never be paid off. Even if they were to find a buyer to buy, they would still be short about $175,000 without considering the selling expenses, like the broker's commission and other normal expenses. So like many people who are "upside down" on their mortgage, the Gonzales family needed an answer.

Now let's meet Paul and Gina Schwartz. Paul and Gina were originally from Chicago, and had moved to Vegas about fifteen years ago. Both their parents had been in the restaurant business, so it was a natural for Paul and Gina to consider opening a chain of sports bars with restaurants when they moved to Las Vegas. It was the right idea at the right time. As new neighborhoods began to open, Paul and Gina simply followed the path of progress; they opened up twenty-five locations in five years. Business was good, and most of the debt had been retired on the facilities. Over the years, Paul and Gina had acquired a number of rental homes as part of their financial planning and part of their retirement plan. The rent covered the mortgage, and when it would come time to retire, they figured they would be able to sell the homes for a good profit to fund their retirement. They wanted to leave the restaurants to their children, not sell them. However, now with the market for homes in a steep decline, there was a question if they would ever be able to sell the homes for enough to cover the mortgage balance, and forget about making a profit. True enough, the rents covered the mortgage payments every month, but all the equity had vanished and promised no return within their lifetime. This had Paul and Gina in a quandary. They did not know just what to do. They needed help to decide what exactly could be the best course of action for them to take.

We need to find an answer for both families, and we will. But before we go there, let's ask one more fundamental question. So just how did all this happen? We'll find out as we read the next chapter.

CHAPTER TWO

So Just How Did All This Happen?

THE DECADE OF THE NINETIES saw tremendous growth of the American economy and stock market. Much of this was fueled by the growth of internet stocks. If you had an internet company and you wanted to take it public (by offering the sale of stock to the public), you were almost guaranteed to make money, whether your company or your products were any good or not. Investors were on a dot. com bubble that continued to grow larger and larger until, finally, in the year 2000, the bubble burst. The dotcom stocks stumbled and prices fell sharply as the market corrected itself.

Large, institutional investors control much of the stock market today; they control large sums of money, and they can move entire markets very easily with just a few clicks of a computer mouse. When the dot.com bubble burst, the larger institutional investors withdrew most of their money from the market to prevent further loss. Most of this money was temporarily parked in money market accounts or other relatively safe low-yielding instruments that would keep the investors from suffering further loss. While this was a natural phenomenon, it was not an action that made the Wall Street brokerage houses very happy. When the money is not in the market and is not being traded on a regular basis, the Wall Street brokerage firms don't make as much money because the trading commissions are few and far between.

So Wall Street had to come up with a solution to attract the larger institutional investors and their money back into the market. What has traditionally been the safest investment in America? Well, traditionally for decades it has been the single-family home. Even in tough economic times, the family still needs a place to call home. In the past, those who have made purchases with credit usually let everything go back to the creditor before ever considering losing their home. After all, the family home is leveraged, which means 80 percent or more of the purchase price can be financed while 100 percent of the value appreciates. It is tax advantaged; so all the mortgage interest can be deducted from one's taxes. And it can be enjoyed while equity is building. It can be touched and appreciated. People who buy on credit, and today that is sadly almost everyone, will let the boat go, let the second car go, give up the cruise deposit, let the new furniture go, and let almost anything else go before they let the home go. Or, that is the way it used to be, before 2007. So traditionally, investing in single-family homes has been a good investment. The problem has been that large investors with billions to invest can't very practically go and inspect and actually purchase many single-family homes. So investing in the mortgages on those homes is the next best thing to do. So how did that come about?

The Wall Street wise guys decided that they would create several large trusts to manage large pools of single-family mortgage notes, all nicely packaged and pooled into several trusts with as many as 500 to 900 million dollars of mortgages in each pool. So Wall Street put together the prospectus for the investors complete with a pooling and servicing agreement (PSA), which determined exactly how the pool was to be managed and operated. That document is usually 300 to 500 pages in length.

The trust then solicited investment dollars from investors who would buy stocks and bonds that derived their value from the collateralized mortgage notes held in the mortgage pools. Hence, *derivatives* were created and named such because they derived their value from something else (the collateralized mortgage notes). The idea was wildly successful. Foreign investors flocked to the idea like flies on honey. Finally, this was a method in which foreign investors could actually participate in the "American dream." Hedge funds, investment banks, foreign pension funds, and even foreign governments, such as Greece, Iceland, Spain, and others, all took large positions in the derivatives market.

Derivatives are different from a stock or a bond that is regularly traded on a visible stock exchange. On an exchange there is transparency, a market is created, the numbers of shares traded is known, trading and pricing history are available, price earnings ratios can be examined, etc. Derivatives have no such exchange. Oftentimes, sales occur in conference rooms, away from the all-seeing and accounting eye of the public. Nonetheless, once the purchasing frenzy of derivatives was afoot, it gained in speed and momentum almost every day. The

Collateralized Mortgage Obligation (CMO) or Asset-Backed Security (ABS) market size and velocity made the earlier dot.com bubble look like a warm-up exercise by comparison.

So, starting in 2001, Wall Street found itself engorged with billions of dollars of cash from investors who had bitten on the prospectus and had invested. Now Wall Street had to go out and get those single-family-home mortgage notes collected into the various trusts that had been established by the Wall Street firms such as JP Morgan Chase, Merrill Lynch, Lehman Brothers, Citibank, Deutsche Bank, HSBC, Wells Fargo Bank, and many others, just to name a few. There were many others, but they were not so familiarly known.

Wall Street's task was to turn all those billions of dollars into mortgage notes. But most Wall Street brokerage houses were not even licensed in the mortgage business. So how was this to occur? No problem. Wall Street would simply use the services of the national lenders, who were, in fact, licensed and equipped with offices and willing employees happy to serve and earn those commissions. So in actuality, the big push for the availability did not come from a hungry American public as much as it did from Wall Street, who needed people to borrow money and sign mortgage notes. The mortgage notes would then be sold on Wall Street, sometimes as many as five or six times, and generate a profit on each sale. It was not uncommon for a $300,000 mortgage note to generate a $400,000 profit from just a few sales. No wonder Wall Street was so eager to see the money loaned out to anyone who would sign the papers. A mortgage note was the source of great profit on Wall Street.

Wall Street's marching orders to the national lenders such as Countrywide, EMC, Indymac Bank, GMAC, Washington Mutual, and many others was to simply lend the money to anyone willing to sign the papers. Wall Street made sure the mortgage officers of the national lenders were well compensated also, with the payment of Yield Spread Premium bonuses just to keep the pipeline flowing. It really did not matter if the signatories on the documents, otherwise known as "borrowers," were qualified to borrow and repay the money or not. Wall Street simply wanted the notes to continue their wild express business of buying and selling these notes and the derivatives that were generated from the notes.

It was not so much the American homeowner who purposefully went out and determined to purchase more house than he or she could afford. Again, the push to get the money placed came from a combination of Wall Street and the national lenders who were serving them. The analogy goes something like this. Mommy and Daddy take little two-year-old Tommy to the candy store. Once inside the candy store, Mommy and Daddy take all the lids off the candy jars and point out some of the best candies to Tommy. Then the parents tell Tommy they are going away for a couple of hours, but they are going to leave Tommy in the candy store. So their last instruction to Tommy is to "not eat too much candy." In a situation like this, obviously Tommy gorges himself until he is very sick. So whose fault was it that Tommy ate too much candy? Was it Tommy's fault, or may it have been his parents' fault? I'll let you provide the answer to that question. I already have my answer.

To facilitate its end result, Wall Street and the national lenders (sometimes known as "pretender lenders," because most of the time from 2001 until 2008 they were not loaning their own money) were lending the money from Wall Street (and its investors) by means of all kinds of "lending techniques." Most of the long-established underwriting standards were conveniently thrown out the window. Adherence to qualifications like sufficient income, debt-to-income ratios, sufficient assets and personal net worth, credit scores, etc., were all discarded. So now we have the advent of mortgages that have never been seen before. Mortgages like the "no doc loan," which basically means that the borrower does not have to document his income or much of anything else. The first cousin of the no doc loan was the "stated income loan," which was a loan whereby the borrower, but in actuality more often the borrower's mortgage representative, simply wrote an income amount on the mortgage sufficient to ensure the loan would be approved by the "desktop underwriting" computer systems that were in place and used by so many large and small lenders alike. Usually, the borrower was not aware of the made-up income number that the mortgage representative wrote onto the mortgage application. The number was the one that was required to get the loan approved, and often was highly inflated. This was self-serving mortgage fraud by the commission-hungry mortgage representative. Of course, one cannot forget the "NINJA loan" which was a loan in which the prospective borrower had no income, no job or assets. Many NINJA loans were approved from 2001 until 2007.

Credit scores were regularly manipulated. Loans were essentially made to anyone with a pulse. One actual client was a waitress in Texas whose income averaged $5,000 per year for the two years immediately preceding her taking a loan. Nonetheless, she was "approved" for a $100,000 loan to purchase a home. Her monthly payment was only 175 percent of her monthly income. A normal standard would be 28 percent of one's monthly income. So she was only 600 percent over normal underwriting standards.

Wall Street arranged and packaged the mortgage notes into bundles that were pooled according to the pooling and service agreement. There were several layers of loan according to type, either prime or subprime, as well as according to loan-to-value ration and credit score. These layers are often referred to as *tranche*, which is a French word meaning "slices." The tranche may be thought of as layers of an onion. The outside tranche may require a credit score of 720 or 740. These mortgages with a borrower having this good of a credit score were rated as AAA. Interestingly, it was actually Wall Street who developed the rating software for the use of Moody's and S&P, the two primary rating agencies who were called in to "rate" the derivatives; thus giving them a cloak of credibility. Usually only the outside tranche were shown to a prospective investor. However, the inner tranche were often with credit scores below 600 and some even closer to 500. These credit scores were already from the start insufficient and Wall Street knew that many of these loans would go into default. If they weren't going to default in the normal course of time, it was almost certain that many of these loans would go into default when the interest rate adjusted up and the monthly payments increased, sometimes by 50 to 100 percent. This projected increase was sold as a plus to the investor who thought he would improve his yield when the payment increased. Actually, it was a negative because now the investor could get nothing as the loan went into default instead of getting a higher yield. Wall Street knew many of these loans would go into default; in fact, even in the PSA there were provisions written into the agreement on how defaults would be handled.

Wall Street knew that many of the loans would go into default; but rather than see that as a negative, Wall Street decided to capitalize upon that event and use it as an additional profit-generating opportunity. Wall Street persuaded AIG and others to write insurance on the mortgage notes. This way if the loans defaulted, Wall Street could collect the insurance, and not have to wait for the full running of the mortgage term to make all its profit. The full term could be anywhere from five to thirty years. AIG was duped by the rating agencies, which rated many mortgage notes based upon 500 credit scores as AAA notes. The rating agencies were paid handsomely for their work. Everyone was making money, so why make waves. "Just keep swimming and keep on making money," was the mentality of many.

One must understand that many of these loans were based upon a teaser interest rate. That means that the loan would normally carry a standard interest rate, for example, say 6 percent. However, for the qualifying and for the first two to three years, the borrower may only be paying 1 to 2 percent. This way it was easier to get more loans approved. When the loan adjusted up to the standard rate, Wall Street knew there would be a flood of defaulted loans. That is exactly what began to occur in 2006 and 2007 as the adjustment triggers began to be pulled. As the defaults occurred, the insurance was called upon. AIG woke up one morning and found they were about 20 billion dollars short. Even Wall Street had begun to sell paper short (that is, betting on the future fact that the loans would, in fact, default). Wall Street had created the paper, and now Wall Street was betting the paper would fail. Certainly, that was interesting if not even criminal. For an in depth insight into this, read Michael Lewis' book, *Big Short*. You may also see the movie by Charles Ferguson entitled, "Inside Job." Another way in which these loans were insured was through something called "cross default swaps." A huge market was created involving the trading of these cross default swaps. One wonders where the conscience was for the people working on Wall Street as they were essentially raping the American homeowner. As Lewis points out in his book, if one incentivizes wrong behavior enough, it becomes possible and even normal for those who are so incentivized. The guys on Wall Street were less interested in what was right and what was wrong, and they were more interested in why their colleague in the next work station made a $500,000 larger bonus than they did. Just to give some insight into the amount of money being made by the Wall Street guys, we will look at one instance that is described in Michael Lewis's book. According to Lewis, an employee of Merrill Lynch by the name of Howie Hubler lost nine billion dollars ($9,000,000,000.00) of investors' money in one day. For that performance, Mr. Hubler received a personal bonus of twenty-five million dollars ($25,000,000.00). It is reported that the head of the Federal National Mortgage Administration (known as Fannie Mae), one Franklin Rains, received a bonus of one hundred million dollars ($100,000,000.00) for his performance before he was fired for ineptness, but he was allowed to keep his entire bonus. Other sources say it was only $90 million. You can take your pick. So where did the money come from to pay these kinds of bonuses to thousands of employees working on Wall Street? You guessed it. It came straight off of the backs of the hardworking, American-home-owning public.

And if that was not enough, when the banks and investment companies on Wall Street blew it, and were about to go under, our illustrious politicians in Congress passed an eight hundred billion dollar ($800,000,000,000.00) bail out to rescue these greedy financial rapists. The financial institutions were considered "too large to fail." So while the Wall Street executives enjoyed the high life in the Hamptons of Long Island, Mr. and Mrs. Smith of Main Street America were literally being put out on the street. Our grandchildren will be paying taxes for decades to come to pay for that bail out event. That money was referred to as the Toxic Asset Recovery Program (TARP for short.) The money was supposed to be used to shore up failing mortgages, but in fact most of the money is still "unaccounted for," but off the books most of it was used for banks to purchase other failing banks and pay bonuses to executives.

As the markets began to fail, you may recall hearing about the near collapse of Iceland, or Spain, or Greece. These were governments that had invested heavily into the Wall Street derivatives market. But one must understand that greedy Wall Street was not satisfied just to rake the flesh off the backs of the American working public. Wall Street figured to make money off the investors as well. It is reported that sometimes an investor, be it a hedge fund or a foreign investor, would give Wall Street an amount of money, say $800,000.00., and was looking for a return of, perhaps, 6 percent. Well, 6 percent of $800,000 is $48,000. However, instead of giving the investor mortgage notes worth $800,000, Wall Street would give the investor mortgage notes worth only $300,000 but bearing an interest rate of 16 percent. You see, 16 percent of $300,000 is $48,000. But the question is, "What happened to the other $500,000 of investment capital?" ($800,000 – $300,000 = $500,000). Could the money have been simply "taken" by one of the largest Wall Street investment banking companies? It is thought by some that firms like this have quietly put away offshore some fourteen trillion ($14,000,000,000,000.00) dollars from the time period of 2001 until 2007. That is money that will be slowly brought back onshore little by little as "earnings." So it wasn't only the little guy that was mugged in the streets by Wall Street. Some of the unwary, unsophisticated investors were equally mugged as well. All of this seemed to occur under the all-too-blind and forgiving and cooperating eyes of the people in American government and Congress, many of whom have been well donated to in their political campaigns by the same Wall Street firms.

So perhaps by now you are beginning to not only understand how but also why all this happened. It was a well-designed and craftily executed plan from the very beginning. The primary motive was greed. The primary method was one of arrogance, with Wall Street simply choosing to believe it was above the law, and could do and get away with anything it wanted to do, regardless of law, rule, regulation, moral value, or otherwise. Money was going to be made, and the more the better. So what if people's lives were going to be wrecked and relationships ripped apart? Little Tommy in the candy store should have known better, even if he was only two years old. He ate the candy. He got sick, and it was his own fault. Screw you! Tough luck buddy! Take your lumps while I enjoy the high life. That was and is the attitude of many who profiteered during their years on Wall Street.

The Mechanics of Fraud

Before we move on, let's look at some of the specific techniques that Wall Street and the banks and mortgage lenders have been using to carry out their criminal fraud against the American public.

By the combined efforts of political leaders, economists at some of the major universities, and business leaders from Wall Street, the Glass Steagall Act was repealed in 1999. This act was a banking regulation act that prevented banks from investing depositors' funds into Wall Street investments. This act was originally passed for the protection of the consumers in our country. It was replaced with the Gramm Leach Bliley Act, which allowed banks to invest in Wall Street investments, particularly mortgage-backed securities. A typical thirty-year mortgage will return 350 percent in thirty years. For example, if you borrow $100,000 with interest, then you will pay back approximately $350,000 over a thirty-year period (which includes the interest and the principal). Now with the ability to make loans and sell them immediately to Wall Street, the banks and lenders found that they could make 150 percent or more almost overnight. This then motivated the banks to make as many loans as possible to boost their profits. As greed and the desire to make greater and great profits continued, the banks and lenders began to relax their lending standards more and more. Pretty soon almost anyone could obtain a loan without having the normal qualifying standards of assets, credit score, and income to show the ability to repay the loan. The banks only wanted to get the loan note sighed so they could sell it without any real risk to the bank or lending institution because it was going to be sold for an immediate profit to Wall Street. Oftentimes the loans were pre-sold even before they were made.

Here is where the fraud enters in. The law of real estate law governs mortgages and/or deeds of trust, and loan notes. However, the law of negotiable instruments governs stocks and bonds and derivatives, etc. Well, when the loan notes were sold to Wall Street they were permanently converted to stock, bonds, and mortgage-backed securities. Hence, real estate law no longer covers the now converted loan notes. However, real estate law still governs the real property of the borrower. Here we have a great divide. The banks and lenders have tried to fraudulently pretend like there has been no divide. However, the divide cannot be denied, nor can the ramifications of that divide.

Real estate law says that if you separate the note (i.e., the obligation or the debt) from the mortgage or deed of trust (i.e., the security and/or collateral for the debt) then the security is rendered void. What this means is that when the lenders sold the notes to Wall Street, the security was separated and rendered void and unenforceable. Even if this were not the case, there are other reasons why the security instruments are unenforceable. For example, the law says that if notes are sold and transferred, then they must be endorsed to be valid. It is similar to endorsing a check in order to have it cashed. Additionally, the law says that if a security instrument is transferred by assignment, then that assignment must be recorded with the county recorder in the county where the security is located.

So what is the impact of all this? It means that when the banks and lenders sold the notes to Wall Street, they ceased to be parties of interest. The note has been sold and has been satisfied as far as the banks and lenders are concerned. Those banks and lenders are now only "servicers" of the debt. They are no longer "owners" of the debt; therefore, they are no longer parties of interest. Only a party of interest can foreclose on a real estate property according to real estate law. So who is the party of interest? One might say that the investors who bought the mortgage-backed securities are the parties of interest, but the sale of those securities operated to "fractionalize" the ownership of those mortgage notes, and they can only be foreclosed upon in their entirety. One cannot bring about a "partial" foreclosure with any percentage less than 100 percent. The mortgage notes were like radishes sent to Wall Street where a giant vat of soup was cooked up and sold. Now who owns that radish? Where is any particular radish, and how do you identify it?

Interestingly, when a mortgage note is accepted into a given mortgage pool, it is attached there permanently. The mortgage pool trustee does not have any ownership of the mortgage notes, so he is not a party of interest. The trust pays no tax on the sale or profit from the notes because it is classified as a REMIC, which is a real estate mortgage investment conduit. The tax liabilities are passed on to the investors. What this means is that when a given mortgage defaults, the loss is passed on to and reported for taxes by the investors. When a given particular note is in default, it is "written off" as a loss with a tax benefit to the investors. When a debt obligation is written off, it ceases to exist.

Since the notes become permanently attached to the REMICs, it is impossible for the servicing lenders and bank to "buy back" a defaulted debt. However, that is precisely what has been happening. The servicing lenders are pretending to buy back the notes and have them "re-assigned" to them. This is fraud. The banks and lenders have been using a lot of forged and bogus document to attempt to produce a fraudulent scheme in the courts to get away with their fraudulent foreclosure schemes.

Even so, remember that when the notes were transferred to Wall Street, the security was rendered void. This means that the debt is now "unsecured" debt. So even if a lender could buy back the debt, it would be unsecured debt and not secured debt. This means that the servicers are essentially servicing unsecured debt. The chain of title has been broken on the debt. The notes were not endorsed, and the security instruments were not assigned nor recorded. Without an unbroken chain of title, there can be no proof of standing as a party of interest with the right to bring a foreclosure. Rule 17 of the Federal Rules of Civil Procedure says, "an action at law can only be brought forward by a genuine party in interest [paraphrased]." So, here we have a situation where there is no party in interest; hence, no lawful foreclosure can be brought by anyone.

The lenders have attempted to use a computer software company to give them the right to foreclose. Mortgage Electronic Registration System, Inc., known as MERS was set up as a private record-keeping company by the lenders to circumvent fees charged by the county recording offices. The lenders have wrongly presumed that by naming MERS as a Nominee Beneficiary on the security instrument that they could transfer the right to foreclose to another affiliated party. However, fortunately, the courts have correctly ruled that MERS does not have any authority to do anything since MERS takes no loan applications, makes no loans, and holds no mortgage notes. Hence, MERS is not a party in interest. One can only give what one has received, and MERS has received nothing (except for a few fees charged to the lenders).

One should not feel too bad or guilty about owning a home where no one can foreclose. Remember, it has never been a "free house" to the borrower. Most borrowers have made down payments, paid closing costs, paid monthly payments, paid real estate taxes and HOA dues, and have made improvements to their properties. On the other hand, the lenders have received full payment when the loan was sold to Wall Street. The lenders have also received profits and fees from Wall Street, they have received bail-out money from the government (which is really just to say money from tax payers; i.e., you and me). Additionally, most of the mortgages were insured by AIG, the FDIC, private mortgage insurance, or by cross-default swaps.

So who is the real loser in these transactions? One might say it is the investors who invested in the Wall Street securities without doing enough due diligence. But there is nothing new about people or institutions losing in Wall Street investment. The real question is whether or not the hedge funds, unions, pension funds, and sovereign nations will bring their own fraud lawsuits against the Wall Street firms who sold them the worthless mortgage-backed securities without fully disclosing just exactly what was being sold. Time will tell, but already we are beginning to see and hear about more and more lawsuits of this type.

It is worth adding that mortgage securitization when it is done properly. Not abused, mortgage securitization does have a valuable place in the American economic system. It can spread risk and allow a greater availability of funds than would be normally available without the ability to spread the risk. However, in this book we are speaking about the abuse of the mortgage securitization system. To understand more of how the system was abused and borrowers were taken advantage of read Exhibit "I," which is the Congressional Testimony of Law Professor Adam J. Levitin from Georgetown University Law School who testified before Congress in November of 2010.

Next, we will look at the practical ramifications of Wall Street's actions and how they are precisely damaging the American Public with the tsunami of foreclosures that are occurring as a result of the planned defaults on the mortgage notes. Who are the prime movers and major players in the foreclosure actions? How are they going about it, and how are they getting away with it? What can be done to stop it? Let's see now, in the next chapter.

CHAPTER THREE

The Loan Servicers Are Doing What?

To fully appreciate and understand how the foreclosure process has been working, one needs to first look a little further at the business model that Wall Street was using. Once the pretender lender had arranged for the "closing" of the mortgage transaction, the money was wired from an account, usually in New York, and the loan was complete. This is referred to as "table funding." Rarely did the Pretender Lender use their own money, and if they ever did, then the money was quickly reimbursed to them in a few days or a few months at most. The mortgage note was then passed through a number of middlemen who were working in the entire securitization chain of mortgage financing. First the note would go to an aggregator, whose job was to accumulate all of the mortgage notes. From the aggregator, the mortgage note would make its way through a Special Purpose Vehicle and then sponsors, depositors, and rating agencies before landing in a pool of notes managed by a trustee. The trustee did not own the notes, but only managed them. This is a key distinction. There would be major IRS consequences if the trust actually owned the notes. When the notes would be sold, there would be large tax consequences. By having the trustee and the trust only "manage the notes," the tax consequences are avoided. With the notes in the mortgage pool, the trust then sold stock and bonds to investors with the value of the stocks and bonds being derived from the mortgage notes as collateral. A particular note was like a cookie that was sent to New York where it was quickly crumbled and the crumbs were sold all over the world. Or to give another picture, think of a particular mortgage note as one radish. Wall Street is cooking up a large, 100,000-gallon vat of soup. The radish is sent to New York and is added to the soup. After the soup is all cooked up, then it is dehydrated, placed into instant soup envelopes, and sold all over the world. The question is: where is that radish? Or better yet, who owns the radish now? Therein is one major issue. Only the owner of the debt has the right to foreclose on the debt. In this situation where the mortgage notes were securitized, the ownership of the notes had been fractionalized, so it became unclear exactly who owned any particular mortgage note. To complicate things even more, Wall Street decided that it liked to work with excel spreadsheets instead of the bulky, messy actual mortgage documents. Assistant law professor Katherine Porter's study done at the University of Iowa revealed that approximately 40 percent of the mortgage notes during this period were shredded. Other urban legends speak of Countrywide warehouses full of notes that were burned to the ground. Another tells of finding an abandoned forty-foot semitrailer parked behind a shopping center in New Jersey, full of mortgage notes. Frankly, nothing is very surprising concerning the type of people and the business that was being operated in such a fashion as it was. Trial testimony has revealed that Countrywide never sent the notes to Wall Street most of the time. This is thought to have been an industry-wide practice.

Wall Street was only interested in the mortgage note. The note is the promise to pay. It is the obligation. While a debt can be proven perhaps without the actual wet signature note, nonetheless, the original note is the best evidence of ownership of the debt. The second document that is always executed by a borrower in a mortgage transaction is either the deed of trust or the mortgage document. Depending upon the state and the jurisdictional laws concerning mortgages (either judicial or non-judicial), one of these documents is always signed by the borrower. It is this second document that is the security agreement. It basically says that if the payment is not made on the note in a timely fashion, then the owner of the debt has the right to foreclose on the property and take it as collateral for the debt. However, the law is also very clear that the security agreement becomes void if it is separated from the note. Here, in almost every case, Wall Street did actually separate the note from the deed of trust or the mortgage, as the case may be. Wall Street was only interested in the promise to pay and the payments. Wall Street was not so interested in the actual houses. Besides that, Wall Street already had all the notes insured with AIG or through cross-default swaps, and did not need the cumbersome deed of trust or mortgage, much less the problem of actually dealing with physical structures.

Now, after the mortgage loan had been made and funded, it was up to the pretender lender or someone else who may have received an assignment, to do the actual servicing of the loan. Servicing the loan means receiving the monthly payments, keeping track of the accounting, receiving and paying real estate taxes and insurance from escrow accounts (if that was part of the mortgage), and also sending late notices if payments were not received. Many times the pretender lender was also the servicer, for example like Countrywide Home Loans mortgages would be serviced by Countrywide Home Loan Servicing. After Countrywide was taken over by Bank of America, then BAC Home loan Servicing, LP, became the servicer. One must understand that the servicer typically does not own the debt. The servicer merely services the debt on behalf of someone else. However, for the past few years, servicers have foreclosed on countless numbers of mortgages. These foreclosures are highly suspect as illegal because in most cases the servicer did not own the debt, and did not have a proper chain of title giving them the right to foreclose on the debt. In the beginning, the borrower did not realize what was happening. The borrower knew he had borrowed the money, and owed the money to someone, so usually the borrower just gave up the home not realizing that the entity bringing about the foreclosure was most likely not the true holder in due course (i.e., owner) of the debt. In actual fact, some borrowers could be placed in a position of double financial jeopardy. They have given the home as collateral to one party, then, a second party later appears, alleging and/or proving to be the true holder in due course of the obligation, with the note and claiming an interest against the borrower for the full amount of the outstanding balance on the note. That would not be a good situation in which to be if you were the borrower.

So, countless homes have been foreclosed upon without proper documentation being presented to the court in the judicial foreclosure states, and without being properly challenged in the non-judicial foreclosure states. (I will speak about the difference between the two below.) The pretender lenders were finally caught red-handed, so to speak, when in some cases during discovery it became apparent that the employees who were supposed to be reviewing files for accuracy of proper documentation were signing off on as many as a thousand files per day, five hundred before lunch and five hundred after lunch. That meant that each file was looked at on average for about twenty-eight seconds—hardly enough time to move the file and sign your name much less actually read anything. These people were referred to as the "robo-signers." The FBI closed one attorney's office in Florida for such fraudulent operations. So the public relations campaign of the "moratorium on mortgage foreclosures" lasted all of about ten days. Suddenly then Bank of America announced that now all of its paperwork was in order, and it would be continuing to foreclose as usual. I don't they could even locate all the paperwork in ten days much less review it all. It was just another PR campaign on behalf of the pretender lenders.

As mentioned above, there are two types of mortgage foreclosures: judicial and non-judicial. First, let's look at non-judicial foreclosure. About twenty-seven states, mostly in the western United States, use this type of foreclosure. It works like this: When the borrower borrows the money he actually signs a deed giving the property to a trustee who is supposed to be a representative of the lender. The lender is typically the beneficiary of the trust arrangement, with the borrower being the actual trustee. So the borrower places the property in the trust for the benefit of the lender. Then if the borrower does not make the required payments, the trustee can sell the property for the benefit of the lender. This can occur without the lender or the trustee going to court. That is why it is termed "non-judicial" foreclosure.

By contrast, in the other twenty-three or so states that predominantly use judicial foreclosure, the lender merely records a lien on the property, and if the borrower fails to make payments, then the lender must go to court and get a court order allowing the lender to sell the property. This type of foreclosure is known as "judicial" foreclosure. So when there is a lawsuit to stop a foreclosure it is usually the borrower who is the plaintiff in a non-judicial state, and it is usually the borrower who is the defendant in a judicial foreclosure state. So though the name of the role may change from one state to the other, depending upon the type of foreclosure that is used the arguments remain the same no matter which type of foreclosure method is used (whether judicial or non-judicial). It may also be noted that several states may have both types of foreclosure available, but usually only one is predominant in normal practice.

It is likely that you have heard of MERS, which stands for Mortgage Electronic Registration Systems, Inc. MERS has been in the news and media quite a bit over the past year. MERS is a Delaware corporation with headquarters in Reston, Virginia, near Washington, DC. MERS was started by some of the larger pretender lenders as a way to facilitate the easy and loose transfer of mortgage notes without all the cumbersome documentation and all the expensive recording fees that are normally charged by county recorders each time a note is endorsed or a deed of trust is assigned to a different party. The law clearly says that such assignment shall be recorded within the recorder's office of the county where the property is located. So the verdict is still out for question to determine whether or not the MERS system is actually a legal system that meets the requirements of the law.

The pretender lenders have been naming MERS as a "nominee beneficiary" on the deed of trust. This way, so their thinking goes, if MERS is named on the document, then that is sufficient for any other entity as long as that entity is a member of the MERS system, to then foreclose on the property. MERS, you see, is basically an electronic record-keeping system to track loans and loan documents. MERS takes no loan applications. MERS loans no money. MERS has no risk of loss, and MERS does not hold any mortgage notes. In fact, all of this is included in the contract that MERS has with its subscribing and paying members. MERS guarantees not to hold any notes; otherwise, the pretender lenders could not name MERS as a beneficiary on the deed of trust.

For awhile, this system worked for the pretender lenders. Today, there are about sixty-eight million mortgages in the MERS system. However, it has been decided by several State Supreme Courts that MERS is NOT, in fact, a party of interest to any mortgage, and, therefore, MERS cannot initiate foreclosure action against anyone. Kansas, Arkansas, Nebraska, a federal court in Nevada, and others have agreed with this conclusion and this line of reasoning. MERS has cheated the county recording offices out of billions of dollars of recording fees that should have been paid by the pretender lenders to the counties.

The deed of trust is actually a contract that says that the trustee, or the newly substituted trustee, can bring a foreclosure action against the borrower for nonpayment on mortgage debt at the initiation of the beneficiary. However, more and more courts are siding with the issue, that if MERS is not a party of interest in the mortgage transaction, then MERS has no standing to initiate anything against the debtor. In many cases MERS has attempted to "assign" its rights to others, such as the pretender lenders. However, one can only give away what one actually has. This is a key element, and a key question. Does MERS have legal standing to do anything? Different courts and different judges have different opinions.

Loan servicers are doing what? That's right. The loan servicers who have been collecting the monthly payments from the borrowers are now beginning to foreclose, as if they actually owned the debt and are the true holder in due course of the debt obligation. In most cases, nothing could be further from the truth, as we have seen with our description of the securitization process involved with the collateralized mortgage debt obligation (CMO). In most cases it is not clear at all, first, who owns the debt, and, second, how much is actually owed. However, this has not stopped the pretender lenders from foreclosing at all. Loan modification is just a PR campaign for the most part, at least for most of the pretender lenders. The pretender lenders will say they cannot talk to you unless you are at least two months behind on your mortgage payments. They'll say, "So please stop making your payments. Next, send us three months of payments as a trial, then we will disapprove you, then we will steal your house through mortgage foreclosure. By the way we are going to add interest, penalties, late fees, BPO (broker price opinion) fees, legal fees, and many other charges to your loan. And Mr. and Mrs. Borrower, what is your alternative? You can continue making payments on a mortgage that is probably twice the amount of the current value of your home." Nice little catch-22 for you, and big profits for your "friendly" bank or pretender lender who is continuing to steal from you with the $800 billion bailout money of your future tax dollars that are currently keeping his doors open to do his dirty work.

Again, recommended reading is the material in Exhibit "I," which is the Congressional Testimony of Law Professor Adam J. Levitin given before Congress in November of 2010. This will help you understand what we as a country are dealing with.

So now the question is how do we stop these crooks in suits from coming and stealing our homes? It is as if Al Capone and Jesse James show up at your front door with guns drawn. They say, "Whiskey and trains are getting a little old. Now we are doing houses. So put your hands up and hand over the keys—now!" Well, fortunately there are still some ways to stop these crooks from doing their dirty work. The courts are still available, and that is the best place to find a solution to *solve your mortgage mess now*! Let's look at the next chapter and see what might be a good solution for you.

PART TWO

The Solutions

CHAPTER FOUR

Strategic Solutions to Help Now!

WHEN ONE IS IN A BATTLE, one has to be cognizant of the enemy and know what tactics the enemy will use. That is the best way to defeat the enemy, by anticipating his every move. There are at least seven strategies that we will examine to see which will work the best for you. As we investigate these strategies, we will also comment on the behavior of the pretender lenders as we go, so you will be able to anticipate what may occur in advance of that actually happening.

The seven strategies are (1) mediation, (2) modification, (3) litigation, (4) debt relief, (5) short sale, (6) tender of payment, and (7) selective short refinance. Some strategies are far more advanced and helpful than others; nonetheless, we will cover all of them. While some do not give much actual financial benefit, they can give the benefit of time. That is time for you to become educated, do your homework, amass your legal defense fund, and prepare to stand your ground and keep your home. All the while, you are able to remain in your home. I will discuss each of the seven strategies individually and we will begin with mediation.

Solution 1. Loan Mediation

Soon after the mortgage meltdown began, the State of Nevada passed into law a provision that offered the homeowner the opportunity to meet with a representative of their alleged lender and negotiate some change in their mortgage. The cost continues to be a modest two hundred dollars and the homeowner can be represented by legal counsel at minimal cost. The homeowner has to elect in writing within thirty days of receiving a notice of default from the lender or the foreclosing trustee. A date is set for the mediation meeting, and all foreclosure action is halted until that meeting is finished. The process usually requires the mediation meeting to be set in advance by several weeks. This can help to stall the foreclosure process, and gain some valuable time for one to consider the other options and make appropriate preparations. Rarely is there ever any genuine benefit achieved in the actual mediation process itself. Many would say that the entire mediation process was only a political band-aid for the state government to appear that it cared and was offering some help to the beleaguered homeowners and voters! Overall, there has been little, if any, genuine benefit from such mediation meetings. Still, every situation is different, and every lender is different. Too, different programs and different policies appear at different times. The cost is relatively low and an attorney is not required, so mediation may be considered as a tool to attempt to gain *some* benefit and at least gain *some* more time. While an attorney is not required, it is recommended for those truly interested in at least attempting to gain some meaningful benefit in the mediation process. Not having professional representation greatly lessens one's possibility of gaining any true benefit. If one is on an extremely limited budget, then perhaps one should forego the mediation and use the funds for one of the other options we discuss later.

Solution 2. Loan Modification

Loan modification was one of the first solutions to appear when the mortgage mess began. Almost overnight, loan modification shops and businesses began to appear, so it seemed, on almost every street corner. In the beginning there was no regulation and no license requirement. Many former real estate brokers and former mortgage brokers suddenly went into business to attempt to help the panicked public who did not know where to turn. There was also a lot of easy money up for grabs; most loan mod shops charged anywhere from $2,500 to $3,500 for their work. Typically, the loan mod shop would ask the borrower for copies of all their loan documentation, and a check. Then the loan mod company would simply call the lender of record or the servicer and request a loan modification. The loan mod company usually did not have any legal representation, and, therefore, had no real legal leverage to get the lender to cooperate; they simply made the request. Nonetheless, most of the lenders were cooperative in the beginning because everything was quite new, the market was in shock and the lenders, at first, wanted the homeowners to stay in their homes and keep making payments. It really did not matter if the mortgage payment was lowered somewhat, so long as the pay period was lengthened, etc. Rarely was there much principal reduction. However, one has to remember that the home values had inflated significantly in 2006 and 2007. The lenders had plenty of room to make at least a little reduction.

However, as time went on, more and more of the lenders began to cease making any real significant changes in the mortgages to help the homeowners. Congress had approved a taxpayer-paid-for bail out for the lenders that strengthened their financial position, and, as a result, the lenders started acting tougher toward the weary homeowners.

A large problem arose for most of the loan modification shops. They had taken a lot of money in from hundreds of clients, but now they were not able to produce much, if any, results. Unfortunately, many of these loan mod shops that had appeared overnight almost like a field of mushrooms, suddenly disappeared just about as quickly. The worst part was that many of them did not refund the clients' money, and the clients were simply left high and dry with no recourse.

Then, fortunately, in Nevada and some other states a well, laws were passed requiring loan modification companies to be licensed and bonded. So, almost all of the loan modification businesses disappeared and became non-existent. The loan modification business was left to attorneys for the most part. Here there was a licensed professional now taking the place of the unregulated and unlicensed person before, but not much really changed. Even though the attorneys had the ability to sue the lender, most of them had not been trained to know what to look for or to understand the primary issues involved in loan securitization. So once again, the consumer was left with a poor option. Again, the borrower was paying $2,500 to $3,500 to an attorney who was not able to gain much true benefit for the borrower. Most of these issues have never been taught in law school since this is the first time in modern history that we have had such a tsunami of mortgage defaults as a result of the securitization machine created by Wall Street.

In actual fact, the homeowner himself is able to conduct a modification directly with the lender. It is not truly necessary to hire and pay an attorney to conduct the modification. What is usually involved is first writing a hardship letter that explains why the payments have not been made. Things like job loss, death, divorce, loss of income, and other extraneous circumstances are all good to include regardless of the borrower's situation. Then a budget of income and expenses is included with the letter. Then tax returns are included, along with pay stubs and copies of bank statements. If one is self-employed, a six-month profit-and-loss statement is included. Finally, there must be a written request for modification. This is not a difficult package to assemble and send to the lender along with their lender application. There is no real need to pay someone $3,000 to $4,000 to do this for you. The important part is to follow up and call the lender every week. First, to make sure they have all the information necessary to send to their underwriting department, and, second, to keep your case on the radar and not just pushed over into a corner. Remember, the squeaky wheel usually gets the oil. Persistence is priceless. Make sure that you only send copies of everything; do not send any originals. Lenders are notorious for losing applications and other documents. Normally, you will be told that it takes at least six weeks to receive an answer. It is very important that you continue to call the lender at least once each week to check up on the status. It is also very important to keep good written records of all conversations, including the date and time, the person spoken to, and the content of the conversation.

Important! Now, if you are already in the foreclosure process, be sure to do this! You must realize that the modification and foreclosure departments of a lender do not necessarily communicate with each other. They have, in fact, different agendas and different motives. So here is what you have to do. You must call the modification company every week for an update on your file. You now must also get the phone number of the foreclosure department. Call the foreclosure department and request that they postpone any foreclosure sale until you have an answer regarding your request for a loan modification. Many times it can take four to six months or even a year to get a final answer on your request for a loan modification. Meanwhile, you are living in your home, not making mortgage payments, saving cash for your legal defense fund (important), and prolonging the entire situation. This is okay. You must remember that the company trying to foreclose on your home has no loss. They did not lend out any money on your home in the vast majority of the cases. If they did lend any money on your home, the loan was most likely sold into a securitization pool, and that lender has already been repaid on your loan from the loan sale proceeds they received shortly after your loan was made. If your loan is in default, then the lender may have already been repaid by mortgage insurance (the premiums of which were paid for by you), by TARP, or by some cross-default swaps, etc.

A word of warning to the wise is in order. Please don't get your hopes up too high for the loan modification with the lender. Most modifications are not approved. There can be many reasons, such as insufficient income, lack of true hardship, lack of lender cooperation, and others. You have to remember that the lender really wants to foreclose on your home. They make more money that way then they do by modifying your loan. I will explain that later, but for now just realize that it is likely you will be turned down for your loan modification request. That is okay. The benefit that you are looking to realize in playing the game is to buy some time, which takes the immediate pressure off of you and your spouse and your family. One has to have a long-term plan and also a short-term plan in dealing with this situation. The loan modification activity is a good short-term plan. And while it is unlikely that you will receive any true benefit from the loan modification, it is not altogether impossible. Occasionally, some people have received a decent modification. Usually it consists of lowered payments, and only rarely does it include a reduction of principal. The thing to realize is that laws and policies can change at any time, and it is worth being in the game just in case something does come along that will benefit you.

Here is a second word of warning to the wise. Most if not all loan modification agreements include, typically somewhere near the end of the agreement, a waiver whereby the borrower waives any and all legal rights and causes of action against the lender. Kind of sneaky, huh? Your friendly corporate lender just thought he would cover his butt from a lawsuit while he was so kindly modifying your loan. Now your thirty-year mortgage is a forty-year mortgage and your lender is sealed off and protected from any litigation. Or, is he? Good question. Fortunately, with HAMP modifications there is no waiver.

Some have argued that since the pretender lender does not own the debt, they do not have the right to modify the debt. Consequently, they also do not have the right to ask for any waiver in an agreement that is void because, again, they do not own the debt. One can also argue that if they do not own the debt, they do not have the right to modify the debt or short sale the property or even foreclose on the property in the first place. Yes, very interesting, indeed. Any waiver in any loan modification agreement that you may have signed can certainly be challenged in a court of law along with any other cause of action that may be brought later on.

Supplemental Directive 10-02

There is one technique that can be helpful in the loan modification arena. If you Google "Supplemental Directive 10-02," you will find a thirteen-page document that most lenders have agreed with in relation to the US Treasury. This agreement says that if a homeowner has a HAMP loan mod in process, the lender cannot foreclose until a decision has been rendered on the application. Even if the application is denied, the homeowner has thirty days to appeal. If the appeal is lost, then the homeowner can make a new HAMP application. This can work well to extend the time for the homeowner to accumulate cash for legal expenses or explore other opportunities.

To make sure this technique work, the homeowner must send a copy of the modification documents along with a letter that points out that no foreclosure is possible (or legal) so long as there is a HAMP modification in process (i.e., the homeowner has applied for a HAMP modification and is awaiting an answer) to the foreclosing trustee. The homeowner must also make sure that the HAMP is applied for more than eight days before any foreclosure date. Also, it is always good to use certified mail (with a return receipt) for keeping good records.

Normally, you will probably not want to sign and accept the final modification agreement, if, by chance, it is approved, which is rare. The main reason for not signing a modification agreement is because of the waiver. However, if you are one of the lucky and blessed ones who by some stroke of providence actually receives a good, decent, meaningful modification, then after you have had an attorney review it (say for a one-hour [only] payment), you may then want to consider accepting and signing it. You must think about it from every angle. You must think not only about today, but think about what will occur in five or ten years. What is your housing market like? What will prices be in five or ten years? Will your house still be under water debt-wise? What are the alternatives? How important is it for you to stay in this particular house? What are comparable homes renting for in your neighborhood? Can you save more by renting, or by staying in your home? If you want to sell in the near term, will you have a mortgage deficiency? Is a short sale a better option? There is no one-size-fits-all answer to any of these questions. These questions include decisions only you can make about your own personal life. However, don't just throw up your hands and give up. Remember, we have four other options to look at. You must finish this book before you make any final decisions, right? That's our agreement. You have more to learn about, specifically all the additional options available to solve your mortgage mess!

So in summary, while the loan modification may not generate any real benefit for the borrower, it can generate the benefit of additional time. Usually, during the approval period, the foreclosure can be delayed as long as you are communicating regularly with BOTH the modification department and also the foreclosure department. If you want to actually get a modification approved, then it is important to show on the application that your household income is negative with the original mortgage payment amount being paid. . In completing the worksheets for the application, try to maximize the income and reduce the expenses as much as possible. Lowering food costs to one hundred dollars per month per person is acceptable, for example. Leave cable TV and other such discretionary items off of the expense list. Additionally, it is important to establish the current market value of the home as low as possible. Finally, one needs to show that with a new modified lowered mortgage payment the household will now have a positive cash flow. One last comment, there is a Net Present Value test that is important to pass. This NPV test can be found online and worked through before any application is sent to the lender or its servicer. Sometimes the test is referred to as the REST report. The last thing to mention is that one has to be persistent and call at least once a week to follow up on the HAMP application. Always keep full notes of each conversation. Note the names (and phone extensions and employee identification numbers, if available) of everyone spoken with and note what they each said. HAMP may not apply to loans that are owned by Fannie Mae and Freddie Mac. However, there are other programs that can be researched for borrowers whose loans are owned by those government-sponsored entities (GSEs). See the HAMP application in the exhibits at the end of this book.

How to Find Out a Sale Date for Your Property

Now, if you have received a notice of default, you will find on that notice something called the "trustee sale number." Usually it is written as "T.S. No." and is followed by a series of digits and characters. Also, on the notice of default there is usually an 800-telephone number for automated information regarding upcoming trustee sales of properties at foreclosure auctions. Call the 800-telephone number and listen to the automated instructions. Then enter the T.S. number and find out if your property is scheduled for sale. In addition to this method, you can usually enter the T.S. number on the website of the selling trustee to determine if your property is scheduled for foreclosure sale. A third method to check on the status of a sale is to telephone the selling trustee directly and ask them the status of your home. Normally, they will only talk to the borrower (you), unless permission has been sent to them authorizing someone else to inquire for you.

So far we have considered the loan mediation and also the loan modification. There are at least five more strategic solutions we must examine. Let's do that now.

Solution 3. Litigation

Litigation is just a fancy word for "lawsuit." But litigation is probably one of the best ways to actually stop a foreclosure and receive some genuine relief from your mortgage mess. In a loan modification application there is usually no legal leverage to get the lender to do anything. However, with litigation, one can back the lender into a legal corner and get some genuine results. Let's begin to see how all this works now.

The court of law is one of the few remaining places where a borrower can hope to receive some relief from the large, steamrolling banking corporations that have been flattening helpless homeowners mercilessly, with little or no regard for the lives of the people involved. An unnamed retired attorney from Arizona was one of the few people in the beginning who actually understood the issues at hand. This was because he had worked as an attorney on Wall Street during the 1990s and was involved in the creation of the derivative instrument. In addition to his understanding of how Wall Street was working in regards to the securitization of debts, he also practiced law and understood how the foreclosure process is supposed to work in accordance with legal statutes and the prescription of law. He was able to see that the basic laws regarding foreclosure were not being adhered to by the foreclosing entities that were foreclosing on behalf of the loan servicers. This attorney filed a lawsuit on his wife's mortgage and fought against the pretender lenders himself. A second attorney from Florida (also unnamed) had worked with the first attorney back when he lived in Florida. This second attorney began to represent homeowners throughout approximately thirty or more states, always using local counsel properly licensed. The first attorney began to teach seminars to attorneys and homeowners, and the second attorney simply took the bull by the horns and met the pretender lenders head on in the courtroom with much success. This all began sometime in 2008. Certainly, there were others, but these two attorneys were pioneers in providing answers and hope to many people.

Additionally, a consumer law expert attorney had already been helping homeowners for years in the bankruptcy courts, which we will address more, later on. Suffice it to say that a round of thanks is owed to these pioneers as well as others who stepped up to the plate with an open mind and willing spirit to dive into a new area of law practice in order to stave off the attack by the large corporations who were attempting to devour as many homeowners as they could, as quickly as they could.

Initially, many of the legal complaints with the courts included a history of how the "securitization process had circumvented the due process of the law concerning foreclosure." This sophisticated description was, unfortunately, beyond the scope of comprehension of most judges, who were overworked and overbooked with bulging dockets as a result of the continuing litigious society. Many of the causes of action were initially based on federal laws that were originally enacted for the protection of the consumer and the borrowing public. These included violation of certain aspects of the Truth in Lending Act, the Real Estate Settlement Procedures Act, the Home Owner Protection Act, the Fair Credit Reporting Act, and others. Some of the other claims involved conspiracy theories involving MERS and the Wall Street crowd, and yet other claims cited violation of the RICO anti-racketeering statutes. Then there were also claims of fraud through lack of disclosure or omission, wrongful foreclosure, breach of either fiduciary duty or breach of a duty of good faith and fair dealing, and unjust enrichment. Also included were demands for declaratory judgment, quiet title actions, and demands for emergency (temporary and permanent) restraining orders. There were numerous other claims that were included, as each case was different even though there may have been some similarities.

Litigants were trying both the state court systems as well as the federal court system. Generally, the state courts have a better reputation for being kinder to the individual, and the federal courts have a general reputation for being more sympathetic toward larger corporations. As time went on, and the legal counsel for the pretender lenders got their act together more and more by the use of template responses, the counsel for the lenders began to remove most of the state cases over to the federal court system. Typically, federal litigation is more expensive and more time consuming. The big lenders figured they could deplete most of the consumers' funds for legal defense, and it did not matter too much to the lenders if they had to spend a few thousand or so to resume their activity of foreclosing on the houses where they had no investment and no risk. The lenders, by their counsel, cried over and over their mantra to the judges, "Your honor, you can't let this despicable non-paying consumer have a 'free house,'" when, in fact, the lenders were doing exactly that very same thing. By foreclosing upon a property they had no legal recourse over (i.e., they made no loan of their money), the lenders were the ones getting a "free house." And that was the very claim that they cried so loud about to the judges all over America, as their attorneys played out the script written for them by attorneys from large firms, in Chicago and Philadelphia and Washington, or by LPS (Lender Processing Service).

While in many ways the court claims against borrowers all made sense, much of them were truly over the head of most of the judges who rarely have time to read all of the daily complaints coming in to them. Outside of the bankruptcy courts, most judges don't even necessarily have a good grasp on the elements of debt, such as what is proper and what is legal and what is not. So while some (especially homeowners) want to allege all of the issues at hand, one has to be somewhat practical in terms of estimating what a judge will actually read, actually understand, and actually be able to rule on in order to turn the case in one's favor.

So as time continued, it seemed that, at least initially in many jurisdictions, the federal judges became hardened against the consumer. There was a certain bias against the consumer in the sense that, "this person has not paid their debt, so they should not continue to live in their house." It has been said by some that the large law firms representing the pretender lenders actually lobbied the judiciary to "educate them on the issues." That may or may not be true, but there does seem to be some rhyme to that reason. The federal judges in the twenty-seven non-judicial states seemed to narrow the case down simply to the deed of trust as a contract. They were less inclined to look at the big picture of securitization, splitting of the note from the deed of trust, and who had standing to bring foreclosure as the true holder in due course of the obligation. So little by little, the state courts seemed to become the courts of choice for most borrowers. Meanwhile, the bankruptcy courts were creating their own history as well, and we will see in a later section of this book.

So for many litigants it seemed that alleging federal violations was just a sure ticket to get the case removed to federal court. You may wonder, *Is there a manner to seek relief from the clear violations of federal law?* Yes, there is. Prior to litigation, assuming there is sufficient time and a sale date is not looming quickly on the horizon, one can use the Qualified Written Request as a way to question the pretender lenders about their practices and their record keeping. We will discuss more on litigation later, but first we want to look at the Qualified Written Request and the Loan Audit.

Qualified Written Request (QWR)

The Real Estate Settlement Procedures Act (RESPA) includes statutory language that provides the borrower the opportunity to request information from the loan servicer regarding the loan of the borrower. See the example attached in the exhibits (specifically, Exhibit A). By law, the loan servicer has to acknowledge the receipt of the request within five (5) days, and has to provide answers to the borrower's questions within thirty (30) days of receiving the request. Be sure to see and use the latest version of the QWR, as provided in the Dodd Frank Act of July 2010. Many times the loan servicers do not comply with those guidelines. RESPA provides for a fine in such case of one thousand dollars, plus attorney's fees and costs. Usually the lender is more responsive to a QWR that comes from an attorney than one from the homeowner. While the servicer may acknowledge the receipt of the request and may actually make a response within thirty days, rarely will the servicer divulge any real information. Usually the questions are unanswered. There are normally three standard responses from the servicers. First, they may ignore the request altogether. This is not good for them, as you can read below. Second, they may simply send you a duplicate set of your closing documents. This is no help, and is a waste of paper. The third response is to deny everything in the request. The request will be spoken of by the servicer as "too broad," or asking "proprietary questions" (the statute says nothing about any aspect of a borrower's loan being proprietary), or asking questions that deal with "trade secrets," or they may write back to simply say they "didn't understand the intent or purpose of your letter and request that you call them should you have any other questions." Of course, that is precisely the point. You are asking them to give you information, please. However, so far, they do not give up such information unless they are forced to give it up in a court of law; hence, lawsuits are filed. The borrower, however, can demand to know who owns his loan, and the servicer must comply with that request.

So while not much information is gained in the QWR, it is, nonetheless, valuable. It allows borrowers to go into court and state that they do not deny that a loan was created; however, they do deny that the loan is owed to the entities that are attempting to foreclose. If a QWR was sent, borrows can show that they have asked the servicer to provide information, and the servicer has refused to divulge that information. This casts a light of suspicion on the servicer and all those connected with them.

Loan Audits

Forensic mortgage audits: Before sending the QWR to the loan servicer, borrowers normally obtain a forensic loan audit, better termed a "forensic review and analysis" (performed by a qualified and certified party), to determine and understand just what violations of the RESPA and TILA Acts and others may have occurred. Usually the cost for such a review and report runs from $500 to $1,500 and, as is usually the case, one gets what one pays for. Many loan audit firms have sprung up, as well as many loan audit software firms, and one can pay $500 for a computer-generated report that does not provide much specific analysis of the borrower's actual loan documents. It is truly impossible for a computer to make judgment decisions about what may have occurred in a loan some three to eight years previously. Go Free Network is certified as a forensic mortgage auditor by the National Association of Mortgage Underwriters. Go Free Network does not use computer-generated software to conduct forensic loan review and analysis. Each page of each loan document is reviewed by a specially trained technician and signed off by a certified loan auditor. A minimum sixteen-page report is produced, detailing the specific areas where the lender failed to comply with the legal standards. Questions concerning the qualification of the borrower, fraudulent approval, lacking disclosures, interest rate disclosures, predatory lending questions, and other violations are all covered in the loan review, analysis, and report.

Depending upon the egregiousness of the violations, one may wish to file in the federal court and seek damages simply on the violations. Some have recommended filing especially where the lender is late with their response on either the twenty-day or sixty-day response. In a case like that, one can win the $1,000 fine in a summary judgment because there is no question of fact. Late is late. Make sure to mail to the lender servicer by certified mail return receipt requested, so you have proof of when the loan servicer received your request. One can usually win the fine money as well as the attorney and other costs. If there is sufficient time, one can file a separate suit in the state court to address the other causes of action that are not federal in nature.

The loan audit also serves a very useful purpose in acting something like a road map for the litigating attorney to prepare the complaint against the correct parties. Surprisingly, most attorneys are actually not that familiar with the normal documents executed in a mortgage transaction. A good mortgage audit can greatly assist the attorney to see the issues and draft a strong complaint against the lenders.

Securitization mortgage audit: Related to the subject of loan audits is the "securitization audit." This audit deals with a completely different subject and question. The securitization audit does not delve into the forensics of how the loan was made and serviced. The securitization audit seeks to find the actual note in a Wall Street mortgage pool and the evidence that the loan note was sold, and is not held by the party attempting to bring the foreclosure. This kind of information is very valuable, indeed, as the litigation proceeds and enters into the discovery phase (of the litigation). Securitization audits may cost more than forensic audits because much time is expended looking for the note in all the various mortgage pools, which include loan notes totaling into the multiple billions. A good securitization audit may also include a pictorial description of exactly how and where the loan note ended up, complete with charts and diagrams suitable for use as exhibits in litigation. Fortunately, most securitization auditors will not charge the full amount up front, and will not charge for the report if they do not, in fact, find the note in a mortgage pool. Just because a securitization auditor is unable to find a particular note, does not mean the note was not securitized. As we have said earlier, the vast majority of all loan notes made by national-type lenders between the years of 2001 and 2008 were, in fact, securitized. It was the industry standard during this period.

Each mortgage pool has a cut-off date and a closing date. Any particular mortgage note must have been put into the mortgage pool before the dates expired. Additionally, the "pooling and servicing agreement" functions much like the "constitution" under which the pool is established and operated. A good securitization auditor can often find violations that occurred, and hence rendered the note "not" a part of a given pool. The typical PSA document is often about five hundred pages in length, so there are lots of opportunities to find critical violations, which can be used as evidence in favor of you, the borrower, in a court proceeding.

More on Litigation

Now we want to focus on the particular causes of action that have and can be alleged against the pretender lenders and their cohorts and accomplices to bring about a stop to the foreclosure process and hopefully an opportunity for homeowners to regain some peace and sanity after being at the mercy of the pretender lenders (usually for several months by this time in the process). The light of day breaks ever so sweetly when one realizes that they do, in fact, have something to do to change their situation, they have some measure of control in a situation that until recently seemed helpless.

As always, it is worth noting that no attorney can guarantee any particular result to any client. The attorney does not control the judge or the jury. The litigating attorney must first get past the judge to even get to the jury. I'll say more on that later. All an attorney can do is first, know the law; second, look at the facts of the client's case; and, third, surmise based upon those facts and the track record and precedent whether the client has a decent chance of prevailing. The attorney can in good faith commit to do the best job possible to present the client's case accurately and forcefully in the client's best interest. Someone has said that a good attorney knows the law, and that a great attorney knows the judge. There is an element of truth in that because judges do take an oath to uphold the law, but they are not robots. Each judge will have his own set of perceived notions and his own set of biases and prejudices based upon his own personal background and personal experience.

Litigation is not a fast process. Someone has defined a lawsuit as "hurry up and wait." There is always a big rush in the beginning to get all the proper documents prepared and filed. Then the waiting starts. Typically, for a foreclosure defense case, it takes three to four months to play out, even in a worst-case scenario in which the attorney loses every step of the litigation process. However, litigation can take up to two to three years in some jurisdictions where the court docket is clogged and things progress slowly. So with those time frames in mind, one can see why economically litigation may still make sense for a homeowner. If the homeowner gives up and moves and has to rent a home to live in, he will be guaranteed no equity in that home. The cost of such a move is often no more than the cost of litigation; and the homeowner usually has a good fighting chance of victory and an opportunity to keep some equity in the home. Think of it this way. If you have to move, you will usually have to pay a month's rent in advance. Plus, you may have to pay first and last month's rent as a deposit because by now your credit score will have been damaged by the lender who has reported you as late and in default. Additionally, you may have to pay large deposits with the various utility departments because of the damaged credit score. Furthermore, you'll have the upheaval and expense of moving and the lost time from work or other activities, not to mention the additional stress. So for many reasons, litigation is a good option for the homeowner. Normally, the attorney payments are offset by the fact that you are not paying the mortgage. From an economic sense as well as a stress level and personal sense, litigation is a good choice for most people. The litigant has a good chance to win, and even if the litigant loses, they at least know they tried. They will not have to live with the nagging question in the future, "I wonder if I could have sued and won." If one does sue and wins, then all the better; then it is time to celebrate and be joyous.

Causes of Action in Litigation

Wrongful foreclosure: The law of mortgages and remedies for default is very clear. First, the debt has to be created. That is accomplished with the note, which is the promise to repay. The repayment of the note is secured by either a mortgage or a deed of trust, depending upon the jurisdiction. Twenty-seven states are predominantly non-judicial and use the deed of trust. Twenty-three states are predominantly judicial and use the mortgage. The homeowner maintains title to the property in states that use a mortgage. In states that use the deed of trust, the homeowner signs title of the property to the trustee at the time the loan is made. If there is a default, then in a deed of trust state the trustee simply orders the property to be sold to pay off the note. Where there is a default in a mortgage state, then the lender must go to court to get an order to sell the property to satisfy the debt created by the note.

Regardless of whether the jurisdiction is judicial or non-judicial, it is only the owner of the debt who has the right, and thereby has standing, to come into court and seek foreclosure and sale of the property. If a party is seeking foreclosure as a remedy and that party is not the owner of the debt, then that is a wrongful foreclosure. Just because someone may have a photocopy of documents that were executed by the borrower some years ago, it does not automatically mean that the parties on those copies are the true parties in today's world. As notes are bought and sold, it is the true holder in due course of the debt who has the right to seek foreclosure as a remedy for default.

Default is defined as "a lack of payment where a payment is owed." It is possible that there is a lack of default, if it can be shown in court that no payment was owed to the party claiming default. As well as substantive issues regarding the foreclosure process, there are also procedural processes that must be adhered to as well. For instance, the borrower must receive a notice of default from the correct party, and there must be an actual default.

In the securitization process of the mortgages from 2001 through 2008, many of the mortgage notes were bought and sold multiple times. In many cases it is not possible to determine who the true holder is in due course of the debt. Much of the traditional paper trail associated with mortgage notes and assignments were overlooked or simply not created by the parties who were involved in the securitization process. A study of 1,733 mortgages done on November 15, 2007, by Katherine Porter, associate professor of law at the University of Iowa (now at Harvard), showed that 40 percent of all mortgage notes had been shredded.

Pretender lenders have been foreclosing upon unwary homeowners without one "shred" of evidence that they own the debt.

It is possible to sell a debt to another. However, to be legal and proper the transaction is to be recorded in the county of the location of the property. Also, the note is to be endorsed by one party to another. Additionally, the mortgage or the deed of trust is to be assigned along with the debt obligation as well. In the fast-moving excel spreadsheet world of Wall Street securitization, no one wanted to take enough time to be legal and proper; hence, in most recent mortgage transactions (since 2001) there is an unbroken chain of title, resulting in a lack of record for who has been the owner of the debt from its creation up until the present moment. Usually there are many gaps in the chain of title, and that presents serious problems in determining accurate ownership of the debt. Even the title insurance companies are becoming more and more sensitive to this issue. Many of the larger title insurance companies have begun to balk and become resistant at insuring the title transfers where banks and lenders have taken over properties through foreclosure and want to now sell those same properties to third parties with a "clean title." The title insurance companies know there are many closets full of skeletons' bones in the securitization closets of Wall Street.

One particular activity that Wall Street regularly did left the door wide open for question by litigants in the court. That was to separate the note (that is, the obligation or debt) from the mortgage or the deed of trust, depending, again, upon the jurisdiction (which, in either situation, is the security). Now a serious flaw has entered into the picture. The debt can remain valid without the security, though in such a case there is no collateral for the debt and, therefore, the holder of the debt cannot initiate foreclosure. In essence, the debt becomes a personal property financial instrument. (Real property is concerned with real estate. An investment in a security such as a stock of bond or mortgage backed security is concerned with personal property.) Conversely, if the debt is separated from the debt obligation, then the security becomes void and unenforceable. This is well-established law and can be found in both statute and also in existing case law. In just about every securitized mortgage, the note was sold off to investors via a mortgage note securitization pool offering. If the security had been left behind and not assigned, then the security becomes void and unenforceable. Some have likened this scenario to a cow with its tail. You can separate the tail from the cow, and the cow is still valuable. But in such a case, the tail becomes practically worthless. In this case the cow is the debt, and the tail is the security. For the security to remain valid, it must be transferred along with the debt, and at the same time the debt is transferred, to the same party.

The pretender lenders attempted to circumvent the requirements of the law by naming MERS as a nominee beneficiary on the deed of trust. They had then sold off the note to investors in Wall Street mortgage pool securities, and kept the security with MERS. MERS would then "assign" the beneficial interest to another party, in hopes that the second party could then foreclose. However, many courts have ruled against this practice of MERS by saying that MERS is not a party in interest in the transaction since MERS does not take loan applications, does not loan any money, does not hold any notes, does not receive any monthly payments, and does not have any financial interest in the transaction other than nominal fees it may earn from its clients (the pretenders lenders). State supreme courts of Kansas, Arkansas, Nebraska, and other states, as well as some of the federal courts have ruled in line with this reasoning. Again, only the owner of the debt has the right to foreclose upon a property.

So in summary, the cause of action for wrongful foreclosure can be alleged for many reasons, including lack of standing, lack of chain of title, no party in interest, and a faulty assignment attempt by MERS as well as possible defective or lacking notice from the owner of the debt to the borrower.

Fraud: There are many different ways in which fraud may be alleged in a law case to stop a foreclosure. One of the most glaring and prominent is fraud by omission or fraud by lack of disclosure. In the instance of a securitized mortgage, the parties who orchestrated the transaction acted in concert to bring about a certain end without fully disclosing to the borrower exactly and precisely what was happening. Those parties would be the pretender lender, the title company, the escrow company, the appraiser, the mortgage broker (if there was one), and possibly MERS, assuming MERS was involved in the transaction. To determine if MERS was involved, simply look at the mortgage or the deed of trust and see if MERS is named as a nominee beneficiary. This can usually be found within the first three pages of the document.

The uneducated and unwary borrower thought he was only obtaining a home loan when, in actuality, he was issuing a stock to be sold on Wall Street. This was never disclosed to the borrower. The loan application was made to a certain pretender lender. That pretender lender "approved" the loan. The borrower had a right to rely upon the approval of the pretender lender, and the borrower most likely thought he was actually qualified for the loan since it had been approved. He thought that the pretender lender was putting its own money at risk in the transaction. The borrower did not know that the loan funds actually came from domestic and foreign investors who had purchased stocks and bonds in the form of derivatives sold by Wall Street. Had most borrowers known and understood the true happening of how their loan was funded, most would have stopped and asked questions, and many would have, perhaps, chosen not to take the loan, realizing that the parties making the loan had no skin in the game and absolutely no risk since they were only making the loan to gain the upfront fees. When borrowers would ask, "What do I do if and when this loan interest rate adjusts?" they were told, "Oh don't worry, you can just refinance."

There was a frequent, secondary common fraud that occurred in most of the securitized mortgages that were originated from 2001 through 2008. That was the inflating of the borrowers' income on the 1003 Uniform Mortgage Application without the knowledge or consent of the borrower. Most mortgage agents fraudulently just wrote whatever number was required for the loan to be approved. The borrower rarely, if ever, saw this number. The borrower was usually asked to sign so many documents at closing that there was little to no time to ask any questions about anything. Furthermore, when borrowers asked what the papers were about they were shunned and told that if they didn't just keep signing, the closing process would never get accomplished. Normally, the loan application was slipped into the stack of papers, and was just one more paper to sign on page four. The income was listed on page two. It was normally never seen or questioned at the closing.

It is considered a predatory lending practice for a lender to make a loan to a person when that person is not qualified to repay the loan. Most lenders would ask the borrower to sign an IRS form 4506T, which allowed the lender to see the borrower's income taxes; however, most lenders did not bother to look at the tax income of the borrower, especially because it was normally going to be much lower than what the mortgage agent wrote (again, without the knowledge or consent of the borrow) on the application. It was as if the mortgage agents and their managers did not want to know anything that might cause the loan to be turned down.

Whenever fraud is alleged in a court action, it must be very, very specific. That means that dates, times, names of parties and persons, and the action taken must all be spelled out very specifically to be successful. The name of the mortgage agent is usually found near the bottom of page four of the 1003 mortgage application form. The 4506T document is often included with the documents given to the borrower at the closing of the loan transaction.

I know of one instance that occurred with one of my clients in Texas. A young lady was working as a waitress. Her income for the two years prior to her buying her house was $5,000 per year. She was "approved" for an $80,000 first mortgage and a $20,000 second mortgage so she could purchase a new home for $100,000 with no money down. Lenders are supposed to use guidelines to make loan approvals. The monthly mortgage payment should have been no more than 28 percent of the borrower's monthly income. With the mortgage payments and any other debts included, the total monthly debt payment should not have exceeded 36 percent of the borrower's income. In the case of the waitress in Texas, the lender approved her loan with a monthly payment that was 175 percent of her monthly income. Her loan was certain to fail and go into default. However, everyone from Wall Street all the way down to the local mortgage agent and everyone in between were so greedy and hungry for their fees and commission that no one said wait or stop, and the loan was funded.

Sometime later, after it became apparent that the waitress was not going to be able to make her payments, and was going into default on the loan, she attempted to sell the home to pay off the mortgage with the sale proceeds. Because the new home did not show well to prospective purchases with her old furniture in the home, she decided to move out and attempt to sell the home with the showings being of a vacant home. She thought it would show better to prospective purchasers this way. Well, the same greedy aggressive lender that had made the predatory loan in the first place now added insult to injury. While the home was still in the name of the young lady who worked as a waitress, the lender's agent came and shut off the water, drained all the pipes, winterized the home, and changed the locks by drilling out the existing locks and replacing them with new locks. Fortunately, the father of the young lady found and kept the drilled-out locks. A lawsuit was filed for wrongful foreclosure, and when the father showed the drilled-out locks to the judge, the judge immediately ordered a restraining order to stop any further foreclosure activity by the pretender lender. Yes, sometimes you can get your day in court after all!

Breach of the duty of good faith and fair dealing: A cause of action that is somewhat related to the cause of action of fraud is the cause of action of breach of the duty of good faith and fair dealing. This cause of action is easier to prove than breach of a fiduciary duty. Often the pretender lenders will argue that there is no fiduciary duty between lender and borrower. There is, however, a fiduciary duty between a mortgage broker and his client, the borrower. Nonetheless, even if there is no mortgage broker, there is a duty of good faith and fair dealing between the lender and the borrower. For the lender not to disclose critical information to the borrower is certainly a breach of this duty. And for the lender to omit to inform the borrower of the true nature of the transaction is also a breach of this duty. It is a breach of the duty of good faith and fair dealing for the lender to approve the loan and act as if the funds were coming from the lender when, in fact, the funds were coming from unknown distant investors.

Unjust enrichment: The argument in this cause of action comes from the fact that most mortgage personnel were paid extra commission and "yield spread premiums" for making subprime loans with adjustable rates. Many times this was the case even though the borrower may have been eligible for a better loan with a fixed rate. Also this cause of action can be alleged in the sense that many times the loan would be sold multiple times. It was not uncommon for a $300,000 note to generate a $400,000 profit by the time it had been sold numerous times.

Additionally, one can argue that if the lender has already been repaid from the proceeds of the sale of the loan, then it would be unjust for the pretender lender to also have the opportunity to sell the house and be repaid yet once again.

Declaratory relief: Declaratory relief is always included in litigation, because in these cases the borrower is asking the court to "declare" that the borrower is the rightful owner of record of the subject property and the pretender lender has no legal or economic interest in the property. Additionally, in most jurisdictions, borrowers have the right to know whom they are dealing with in any business transaction, such as a mortgage transaction. The true identities cannot be legally kept from the knowledge of the borrower. So borrowers can sue to find out who is the true holder in due course of the debt. Along the way, they can request that the court make an order declaring that the current pretender lenders do not, in fact, have any interest in the property. The burden of proof remains with the pretender lenders, and most of the time they cannot prove that they own the debt because it is true that they do not own the debt. Declaratory is especially helpful when one is current on the mortgage but has lost significant equity because of the housing crash caused by inflated appraisals during the period from 2001 to 2008.

Injunctive relief: Certainly injunctive relief is at the heart of any borrower's petition before the court. Here the borrower is simply asking the court to enjoin (that is just a fancy word for stop) any further foreclosure activity and certainly any sale of the property at auction or otherwise until the merits of the case have been heard and ruled upon.

Injunctive relief may be included in an initial petition before the court, or it may be accomplished by means of a motion for "temporary restraining order" and/or "preliminary and permanent restraining order," the latter will stop a sale until the case moves into discovery and further on into trial. If there is not enough time for a hearing before a sale date, then a motion for "emergency ex parte TRO" can be made to the court without a hearing. Typically, there are certain requirements that must be complied with for such a motion to be successful. Such requirements include: the borrower will be damaged by the sale, the borrower has the likelihood of success in such a trial, and the other side will not suffer any particular damage as a result of the TRO, and that it is in the interest of good social order to grant the TRO. The arguments in favor of the granting of the TRO are alleged in the Memorandum of Support, which normally accompanies such a motion before the court.

Sometimes the court may wish to ask the borrower to post a bond for the repayment of any potential damage to the other side, such as having to wait to foreclose on a house that they never loaned any money into. We like to argue that the house itself is more than enough security for any "damage" caused to the pretender lender. A judge may ask as much as all the arrearage on the mortgage to be posted as a bond. However, usually the bond requirement is modest and may be only a few hundred dollars.

Typically, a TRO is only good for about two weeks, so it is necessary to also make a motion for a preliminary injunction, which is normally good indefinitely to stop a sale of a property until there is a determination on the merits of who, if anyone, has the right to foreclose. Along with the other arguments, one can argue that additional time is required for discovery to find out the answer to many of the questions concerning the mortgage debt.

Quiet title: This cause of action seeks to set the record straight in the sense that the court will order, similar to a declaratory judgment, that certain entities have no interest in a given property, and cannot come again and attempt to assert any such interest. A quiet title action can be used to remove liens such as mortgage liens off of the county property records on a given property. This way, a property can be sold or refinanced at a later date without the complications of having to clean the title when it is not convenient to do so. This means that the homeowner will be able to acquire and purchase title insurance to give to the new owner if there is to be a sale of the property by the borrower at a later date. Also, if the borrower wishes to refinance at some later date, the new lender will also require title insurance to make sure that the homeowner is the owner of record and that no other parties, such as the pretender lenders, have any interest in the property.

Usually, quiet title is sought initially, but is normally one of the last steps in the litigation process. The celebration of achieving quiet title will not be quiet!

State Court or Federal Court?

Aiding and abetting: Because the pretender lenders and their national counsel prefer federal court much of the time, and because usually the borrower prefers to be in state court, we will now consider how to accomplish a court hearing. If the borrower alleges a number of federal violations of various federal statutes, such as RESPA, TILA, HOPA, and others, then the attorneys for the pretender lenders will rightfully "remove" the case to the federal court on the basis that the subject matter falls under federal jurisdiction. Many times the lender counsel will attempt to remove a case regardless of whether there is federal subject matter jurisdiction of not. Federal court is typically more expensive, more time consuming, and less friendly to the borrower.

So the borrower's counsel must strategize just how they want to plan the case if they want to stay in the state court system. The borrower does have the right to "remand" a case back to the state court if it has been removed to the federal court, but this can only be done for good reason. One additional way in which a lender's counsel can remove a case to federal court is by "diversity of citizenship." This means if there is only one citizen of the borrower's state named in the case, and that being the borrower, then the case may be moved to the federal court. So often, to keep a case in the state court system the borrower needs to do two things. First, do not allege any violation of federal law. Base all claims and causes of action upon state law. Second, name an additional party to the suit who is a member of the same state as the borrower. This could be a mortgage broker or title agent or an employee of the lender, appraiser, or escrow officer. Obviously, there has to be a legitimate reason for naming such a party to the case. One cannot name a party without reason.

This, then, is where one can use the aiding and abetting cause of action as a means of including a fellow state citizen in the case. For example, in the fraud complaint, one can name some of the above-mentioned potential parties as aiding and abetting in the perpetuation of the fraud. For example, there could be no closing of the loan transaction without an escrow company and a title insurance company, etc.

Of course, if the borrower's mortgage agent, or his company, are citizens of the same state, or registered in the same state, as the borrower's state, then one may not need to use the aiding and abetting cause of action to assist to keep the case in state court. Additionally, if one is removed into the federal court system, then one may consider amending the complaint later to include some of the violations of the federal statutes if, in fact, the mortgage audit identifies some of those violations to have occurred at the time of the making of the loan.

Multi-plaintiff suits: A multi-plaintiff suit is a lawsuit where you may have one or more common defendants, such as a lender, a trustee, a nominee beneficiary, a mortgage broker, and a title insurance company, just to mention a few possibilities.

Then instead of just having one plaintiff for each suit, you may *join* multiple plaintiffs who have similar or identical claims against the defendant. For example, all of the plaintiffs may allege fraud by omission, or negligent fraud, or fraud by misrepresentation, and wrongful foreclosure against a common set of defendants.

A multi-plaintiff case is much less expensive than a class action suit because you do not have to notify every member of the class. That could be millions of dollars in postage alone in some of these mortgage foreclosure defense cases. Then the multi-plaintiff case does not have to qualify as a class action suit by the court's approval, as a class action suit does. Another advantage to the plaintiffs is that the cost of the case can be spread over many plaintiffs instead of just one or two.

Actually, the attorney can make more money, and do a better job in a multi-plaintiff case also. No attorney could take on two hundred clients one by one. The cost as well as the amount of time necessary would be prohibitive. Then, too, this would tend to burden the court docket, which is already bulging at the seams. So there is a lot of economy of scale for everyone by using a multi-plaintiff suit. Typically, one suit can be filed against one lender as a defendant, and there can be thousands of plaintiffs. A second case can be filed against another lender, and so on. This way the resources of the good litigating attorney are best used to serve the highest number of clients who need help. Multi-plaintiff suits will most likely be the new wave of the future in foreclosure defense. The need is there. The demand is there. The class action is too expensive. Resources are limited, and the court docket is limited. So bring on the multi-plaintiff suits. Visit **www. SolveMyMortgageMessNow.com** to find an example of a mass multi-plaintiff suit.

Multi-party lawsuits may well be one of the best ways for borrowers to have their day in court. Most law firms doing multi-plaintiff suits will accept payment by credit card, so the homeowner does not have to pay all the cash in one lump sum. The firm may have a success contingency fee at the end of the case, but that is only owed if, in fact, the lawsuit is successful. Payment of the success fee over a period of years or through refinance possibilities may make the payment of that fee easier for the homeowner. Also, it may be that the damage award from the court will require the unsuccessful lenders to pay the contingency fee for the borrower.

Currently, there is a law firm that is suing Bank of America and Countrywide, Wells Fargo and Wachovia and ASC, Citi Mortgage, GMAC, Chase and WAMU, and One West Bank and Indymac. They have said that they will file a suit against other lenders if they have as many as forty plaintiffs to join the suit. To find out more about the multi-plaintiff lawsuits, go to **www.SolveMyMortgageMessNow. com** and select the "Multi-Plaintiff Suits" tab on the website.

These particular lawsuits are based on fraud among other things. So this means that a borrower may join the suit even if their home has already been foreclosed upon, or if the borrower is in the middle of a foreclosure action, or even if the borrower is current on their mortgage payments with no action occurring at the current time. If a borrower completed a short sale without knowledge that the lender had fraudulently cooperated with the borrower in the sale, then the borrower can challenge that sale and seek to have it unwound and stricken from the property records. It would depend upon the judge and the jury whether the suing borrower would receive the return of the property or damages or both.

The law firm can take client borrowers from any state, so there is no jurisdictional limit. This is because the claims are not so much based upon real estate, but rather are based upon fraudulent business practices.

In some cases the lenders have ceased foreclosing upon plaintiffs in these cases because the evidence against them is strong enough that they do not want to increase any damage awards against them by wrongfully foreclosing as well. So while the case is not a foreclosure defense case, per se, it can sometimes work to prevent a foreclosure that might otherwise occur.

Class action litigation: Not much has been done yet in the arena of Class Action litigation, but the time is now and the opportunity is very ripe for some significant class action litigation on behalf of the homeowners. A savvy litigator will choose good clean candidates for his model litigants. These might be borrowers who are still current on their mortgage for example to avoid the charge that the borrower is just trying to get a free house. The clients should appear good, and be able to testify in court in an articulate manner. It helps if they are responsible in society as well, employed, good family people, etc. There can be some who are in default also.

One might choose to actually file in the Federal Court because often it is said that the caliber of the judiciary is better in the Federal Court. Moreover, since the Bankruptcy courts are all Federal, there are many, many good precedent cases in favor of the borrower in the Federal court system.

One of the primary causes of action should be for Declaratory Relief. The homeowner is asking the court to clarify who is really, legally, and truly entitled to receive the monthly payments that are being made. This puts the burden of discovery on the side of the lenders to prove that they are entitled to receive the monthly payments and the mortgage proceeds.

One advantage of the class action is that it limits the number of actual litigating clients for the actual litigation. Many others may be added as members of the "class," but their particulars do not come into play in the course of the actual litigation. This helps to control the amount of paperwork from the other side trying to bury the homeowners' attorney with motions and discovery and depositions in an inordinate manner.

Other causes of action such as fraud and others listed above can be added to the complaint as well. One cause of action to add for sure is injunctive relief to stop any potential sale of the borrowers' homes until the case is settled. One should attempt to obtain this injunctive relief without the requirement of a bond since the property is more than enough collateral for any claims. If monthly payments are required to be paid, then they should be paid into a court trust fund until the outcome to the case instead of being paid to the servicer who position is being challenged.

All research regarding Trust Searches and Reports (see page 60 "Bloomberg") should be done in advance and included in the complaint as exhibits. The stronger the complaint is on the face, the more effective it will be.

The court has to certify the case as a class action. This can be done since the clients can be gathered into suits where they all have the same lender, with similar fact situations, and seeking similar results. The results of the case don not have to be identical for every client as is typical in a class action. Here, one could have the court approve a "formula" that could be applied impartially to every borrower. This way the client with the one hundred thousand dollar mortgage will not have the same monetary damage award as the client with the million dollar mortgage in terms of number of dollars. Nonetheless, each will have an identical percentage relief award even though the dollar amount may be different. The homeowner whose mortgage is rescinded at one hundred thousand will benefit in the amount of one hundred thousand dollars. The client who million dollar mortgage is rescinded will benefit in the amount of one million dollars. The dollars are different, but the result is the same.

Much of the expense of such a suit is in notifying all the potential members of the class. Here, one can ask the court to require the servicers to notify the borrowers by simply enclosing a notice in the monthly payment envelopes that they are sending out on a regular basis anyway. They already have all the names and the addresses, and they are paying the postage also. So, this is the best most efficient way and it transfers the cost to the lenders who are likely the parties at fault in many of these situations with securitized mortgages. If the members of the class are charged a nominal fees by their counsel, many will choose to take advantage of the opportunity and will be happy to make such a payment to get their mortgage mess solved. As time goes on, class members can opt in and join the suit. The focus of the suit is to prove that the servicers and lenders do not own the debt and therefore, have no right to collect payments or to foreclose. The suit will initially name as additional Plaintiffs, John and Jane Does 1- 20,000. As the borrowers opt in, they can be added to the suit.

The complaint will also include a cause of action for quiet title. This way once it is shown that the named defendants do not have any interest in the property, then the rest of the world can be dealt with by means of a notice of publication for a period of time. Assuming, none appear, then court can order quiet title in favor of the homeowner.

The complaint can also include a demand for disgorgement of payments that have been wrongfully made over a period of time. Here the servicers and the lenders or whoever is named and has received payment must return those payments to the homeowners. Punitive damages can also be included in the damage demand. Moreover, the damage demand should include a demand for the attorneys' fees somewhere close to the forty percent level.

With the evidence available, one can make a motion for summary judgment using the Rule 54B statute. This can shorten the amount of time in the litigation, and get the result for the homeowners sooner than would be thought otherwise.

Because this problem is so large and affecting so many families and individuals, there is good reason to move ahead with a class action at this time. For more information on the Class Action Litigation contact the website www. SolveMyMortgageMessNow.com.

Solution 4. Debt Relief

Debt relief is a wonderful-sounding phrase. The other term for debt relief is "bankruptcy." In former days bankruptcy had more of a negative stigma associated with it, but in today's world it is not so much the case. The bankruptcy courts exist simply for the purpose of providing assistance to debtors who are not able to stand up under the load of debt they carry. In the olden days when most of business was straightforward (not so deceptive), there may have been reason for something of a stigma to be associated with bankruptcy. However, in today's deceptive world of mortgage securitization, computerization, and other technological advances, it is easier for the unwary borrower to be fooled and trapped in a situation that was not caused by the borrower's lack of responsibility or work ethic. In much of today's mortgage world the defaults have been, literally, designed by the wise guys of Wall Street. They knew well in advance that many of the loans being made were sure to default. That is even stated in many of the investors' prospectuses that Wall Street used to sell the investors on the idea of investing in the mortgage pools. For example, any time you qualify a would-be borrower on a $2,000-a-month payment, which is a teaser rate with the use of phantom income, and then know in advance that the loan will adjust in a few years to a $3,500-per-month payment, you can be assured there will be a high rate of defaults on those mortgages. Many of the securitized mortgages were designed just so.

While housing values have fallen 70 percent in some markets, with no promise of ever rising to the lofty value heights once experienced, it is essentially financial suicide to continue paying on a mortgage that will never be paid off. Better to just legally walk away from the property and rent a similar house for about half of the mortgage payment on the first house. However, it is not that easy. One cannot just walk away without the potential of incurring a tax event for the mortgage forgiveness, and potential deficiency judgment for the mortgage amount over the current value for which the house can be sold. For example, if the house has a mortgage of $400,000 and can only be sold for $200,000, then the borrower may receive a 1099 for the $200,000 mortgage forgiveness. Then, too, we are speaking about someone's home. This is not just another property. This is a home! There are significant emotional and psychological issues attached and involved with such a decision. Are there school age children? Can the children stay in the same school if the borrower(s) has to move? What message do parents give to their children in all this?

We are going to look at three different types of bankruptcy. The first is Chapter 7, next is Chapter 13, and lastly is Chapter 11. Both Chapter 7 and Chapter 13 are for personal bankruptcy. Chapter 11 is for a business bankruptcy. However, an individual can use Chapter 11 if the income and debt limits are exceeded above the limits in Chapters 7 and 13. Let's get started by looking at Chapter 7 bankruptcy.

Chapter 7 Bankruptcy

Chapter 7 bankruptcy is for the person who wants to "wipe the slate clean, not keep any property, and receive debt forgiveness quickly and start over." That is spoken in general terms. Let's look at how you can also have an opportunity to keep your home, or at least some of the equity in your home. We will deal with that a little later, but first let's look at some of the general aspects of a Chapter 7 bankruptcy. First, it is not available to everyone because there are limits to the amount of debt and also the amount of income allowed to be qualified for this remedy. Not to worry, there are alternatives. The income is determined by a "means test," which is different for different states and different economic areas in the country. There is a chart available online that you can reference to look into this. However, if the debtor earns in excess of the state median income and is able to repay 25 percent of non-priority, unsecured debt, then the debtor will be ineligible for Chapter 7 protection and must file petition using the Chapter 13 process.

No matter which kind of bankruptcy petition is filed, the debtor must complete an online credit-counseling course and receive a completion certificate to be included with the documents to be filed. If this course is not completed and the certificate is not included with the documents to be filed then the petition will be rejected by the bankruptcy court. This course can be found at www.personalfinanceeducation. com as well as www.bkcert.com. The cost is around fifty dollars.

The automatic stay immediately stops the sale of property: When a debtor files for bankruptcy, the debtor's property is protected by the "automatic stay," which prevents creditors from attempting to collect debts without the consent of the bankruptcy court. The Automatic Stay gives immediate protection against foreclosure, repossession of vehicles, eviction from a dwelling, garnishment of wages, seizure of bank accounts, and termination of utilities.

The Chapter 7 bankruptcy process: After the debtor files his documents with the court, he is appointed a trustee from the court. It is the job of the trustee to see that the creditors are paid back as much as possible, and the trustee receives a percentage of those payments, often around 10 percent. Some weeks after the papers are filed there is a "meeting of the creditors." This is a brief meeting, and normally most creditors do not show up. Many times the meeting is less than a half hour, or even only ten minutes. The trustee will organize the debtor's assets into "exempt" and "non-exempt" categories, according to dollar amount and legal definition. Often in a Chapter 7, the non-exempt property will be sold to generate funds to repay some of the debt.

"Secured debt" is debt where there is some collateral attached to the debt. For example, the collateral in a car loan is the car. The car secures the debt to purchase the car, etc. In a mortgage or home loan, it is the home that is the collateral that secures the note for the funds borrowed to purchase or refinance the property. The best example of an "unsecured debt" is a credit card. Money is borrowed, but there is nothing in the form of collateral to secure that debt; hence, it is an unsecured debt.

The entire Chapter 7 bankruptcy process can take from four to six months to complete. There are some debts that are classified as non-dischargeable. Examples of this would be student loans, child support, damage awards for intentional damage, or damage awards as a result of intoxication. One is only allowed to file a Chapter 7 bankruptcy once every eight years.

Fraudulent transfers: Sometimes persons who file a bankruptcy will attempt to "hide" some assets from the bankruptcy court. This is not legal, and can cause one's bankruptcy petition to be thrown out and dismissed from the court. There may be other criminal charges as well. So, any transfer that is made within the last 180 days of filing a bankruptcy petition will be called up and investigated. This is especially the case if the transfer was to a family member, etc. So the best advice is to not try it at all.

Real property in a Chapter 7 bankruptcy: Normally, real property, such as your home or any rental or investment properties are not kept by the debtor who files a Chapter 7 bankruptcy. However, there are two potential ways to work an exception to this normal guideline. In the first instance, there is the necessity of having equity in one's home, which unfortunately most people do not have in today's real-estate-bust economy. However, there may be some that do, so we will take a look at it now. It comes about by using what in Nevada is called the "homestead exemption." This is the amount of equity that is exempt from the bankruptcy that the homeowner is allowed to keep from the court and the creditors. Not all states have a homestead exemption, but many do have such a provision, including

Texas and Florida, just to mention a couple more states. This is how it works. Let's say you had a mortgage of $100,000 and the property was worth $215,000. Let's say the cost of selling the property is $15,000. That means that after the property is sold and the selling expenses of $15,000 plus the pay-off of the first mortgage of $100,000 are both made, there would still be $100,000 remaining. In Nevada, the homestead exemption is anything up to $550,000. So in this case, the debtor would walk away from the bankruptcy with $100,000 in cash.

Now let's look at the second scenario. Here, let's use the same numbers in the example we just used. However, in this case we are going to list the $100,000 mortgage as a disputed debt (i.e., the home value is $100,000 less than the outstanding payoff amount of the mortgage). The burden of proof is on the lender to prove they own the debt. Usually they cannot accomplish that. So, in a best-case scenario, if the lender cannot prove ownership of the debt, and as long as no one else proves the ownership of the debt, it is possible that the judge will allow the homeowner to walk away from the bankruptcy court with not $100,000, but $200,000. That is the total of the mortgage that was wiped out because of lack of proof of claim by the lender, and the $100,000 of equity that the homeowner had beyond the mortgage amount.

Chapter 13

Chapter 13 bankruptcy allows one to have higher limits on both debt and income. Again, the income is determined by the state's means test. It is also affected by whether or not there are dependents. The typical debt limits for the debtor at the time of this writing are $360,000 unsecured debt and $1,080,000 secured debt. However, there is one more category of debt in addition to secured and unsecured. We will refer to this kind of debt as "disputed" debt. One is not bound to the limits above if the debt is disputed. One can also exceed the limits if no one objects. Often the trustee will go along with it because he will make more money.

Chapter 13 bankruptcy involves, basically, a reorganization of the debtor's debt and a payment plan. The debtor must have income in excess of living expenses to be able to make some kind of payment plan. Often only a small percentage of the debt needs to be paid back. It's important to remember that the sole purpose for the existence of the bankruptcy court is to assist the debtor, and the bankruptcy judges have no problem slashing away large amounts of unsecured debt as well as many, if not most, second and third mortgages.

Just as in Chapter 7 bankruptcy, the debtor must complete a credit-counseling course and obtain the necessary certificate; then, that certificate must be included with the documents filed with the court. Again, failure to include this certificate of completion within 180 days of filing bankruptcy will mean that the filing is rejected.

In the Chapter 13 filing, it is the debtor who actually proposes the payment plan. In this regard, it is good to think about a budget that includes all living expenses and some excess to make some repayment on at least some of the secured debts. Depending upon the amount of debt and the amount of money required to repay the debt, the repayment plan can be either a three-year plan or a five-year plan. Of course, the debtor can always pay off the agreed reduced debt sooner, if the debtor so chooses.

There is a trustee is a Chapter 13 similar to the Chapter 7. All payments are made to the trustee who, in turn, distributes to the creditors. Even though bankruptcy may stay on one's credit record for seven to ten years, a potential future credit request with a bankruptcy is looked upon more favorably by a potential lender than a poor credit record with no bankruptcy. The reason is that the future creditor will think that a future borrower with bad credit may later file for bankruptcy, which would result in that creditor not receiving anything. On the other hand, most creditors understand that if a person has already filed bankruptcy, then they cannot file another bankruptcy for eight years. So the person with the bankruptcy on their record is actually a better credit risk than someone with bad credit and no bankruptcy. This makes sense when one thinks about it.

The automatic stay on sale of properties operates in a Chapter 13 just as it does in a Chapter 7. There is also the prohibition against fraudulent transfers in Chapter 13 as well.

Listing mortgage debt as disputed debt: It is important to list any questionable mortgage debt as disputed debt when filling out the bankruptcy forms. Not only does this allow the debtor to keep from going over the debt limits, but it also allows the debtor to challenge the debt ownership in the bankruptcy court. The burden of proof remains with the creditor as it does for all debts in a bankruptcy court proceeding.

Chapter 11

Chapter 11 bankruptcy is normally for businesses. However, if one has too much personal debt and/or too much personal income, such that they cannot qualify for a Chapter 13, then they can file a Chapter 11. The "automatic stay" is still available in Chapter 11. This will stop your home from being sold until after the bankruptcy is filed. It is possible that the lenders will attempt to come into the bankruptcy court to lift (i.e., remove) the automatic stay against foreclosure. That is fine. That presents a perfect situation to challenge them in the ownership or lack of ownership of the mortgage debt.

There was one case in Massachusetts in the court of a Judge Young where Wells Fargo had the first mortgage and Ameriquest had the second mortgage. The borrower had filed a bankruptcy, and the pretender lender tried to lift, or remove, the stay against foreclosure. When it became apparent to the judge that neither of the lenders actually owned the debt obligation, he levied a fine of $500,000 against the two lenders, and a fine of $150,000 against the attorneys of the lenders for bringing fraud to the court. On appeal the fines stuck against Ameriquest and their attorneys.

In a Chapter 11 proceeding, the creditors actually get an opportunity to vote on the approval of the payment plan. In a Chapter 13 that is not the case. Even so, each creditor only receives one vote.

You will want to be represented by good, knowledgeable, experienced legal counsel who will assist you to challenge the ownership of the debt in any of these cases. Additionally, you may need to bring a suit for quiet title against the lenders later to get them to remove the lien from the record of the property. Many of the normal "Bankruptcy Mill" law firms that represent hundreds of clients will not normally be open to doing anything different than what they always do, and so you may not want such a firm to represent you to get the result we speak of here.

How to Keep a Bankruptcy Off Your Credit Record

Some investors have excellent credit scores (say, 800) and also have good cash flow. Nonetheless, at the same time they are still affected by this mortgage meltdown we are experiencing. They need help also. This particular strategy will not work for your personal residence, but it can potentially work for you in regard to any investment properties you own. Think of Paul and Gina Schwartz who we mentioned earlier in the opening chapters of this book. If you recall, they were prosperous and owned several restaurants. They also owned several residential properties that they rented out. Some attorneys are using a strategy that goes like this.

First, a separate LLC (limited liability company) is formed for each property. Then that property is transferred to that particular LLC. Then that LLC can file a chapter 11 business bankruptcy. This way the bankruptcy does not show up on the personal credit of the individual, though it will show the LLC as having filed a bankruptcy. Then one has a few choices. One option is to do a normal Chapter 11, which results in the second mortgage usually being stripped off and some relief on the first mortgage, such as reduced interest for some portion of the remaining debt. The other solution is to list the mortgage debt as "disputed" and challenge the lender in the bankruptcy to prove that they actually own the debt. This may result in a larger forgiveness of the debt if the lender cannot prove they own the debt.

This route may be considered expensive by some standards because the Chapter 11 bankruptcy can cost several times more than a Chapter 7 or a Chapter 13; however, this must be looked at in comparison to the possible benefit that can be gained.

There are other people who are pushing the envelope of ethics by using the bankruptcy courts in yet another way. This is considered questionable by many, but may not be actually illegal. In light of what the Wall Street people have done in conjunction with the lenders, one may find justification within one's own conscience. What is referred to here is that a mortgage debtor will sometimes transfer a 1 percent ownership interest in their property to someone who is already in a bankruptcy proceeding. This is done by a quitclaim deed that is recorded with the county recorder. This is an actual transfer, and has value. If the house is worth $250,000, then the value is $2,500. The person who has filed the bankruptcy then adds the property to their schedule of assets. The automatic stay will then stop any sale of the property. However, this solution is only temporary until the bankruptcy is discharged. So it may be expensive depending upon how much time is gained. But, the money is not money out of pocket. This solution is probably a solution of last resort, where one has no cash to hire anyone to help and desperately needs some time to find a more workable solution. Some unscrupulous entrepreneurs actually overcharge individuals to accomplish all of this. It seems particularly unethical to prey on those who are in desperate straits. Each one has to be led by their conscience. And remember, this book does not give any legal advice. People must consult their own attorneys about anything mentioned in this book. This book is only to get you to think creatively about the possible options and then make your own decision in concert with good legal counsel.

Another potential use of the Chapter 11 solution could be attempted as follows. One can combine the advantages of the multi-plaintiff suit mentioned above with the Chapter 11 benefits. It works like this. A large number of borrowers can transfer their properties to one single LLC (limited liability company). Those who transfer their properties (the borrowers) to the LLC can proportionately own the LLC. Theoretically, the transfer would likely trigger the due on sale clause in the mortgage, which says that upon any transfer of any interest in the property the entire outstanding loan balance is due immediately. Once the lenders attempt to foreclose, then the LLC files for a Chapter 11 bankruptcy relief. In the filing, all of the mortgage debts are listed as "disputed debts." This means that the lenders have to come into the bankruptcy court to prove that they own the debt. The automatic stay will be in place to stop any foreclosure while the adversarial hearing takes place with the lenders attempting to prove they own the debt. Assuming the lenders fail in proving ownership of the debt, then the bankruptcy court can rescind the mortgage debts. There may be some efficiency gained by grouping borrowers with like lenders all into the same LLC. To my knowledge, this strategy has not been attempted yet, but it is an intriguing solution to the mortgage mess.

Solution 5. The Short Sale

A short sale may be defined as, "a sale of a property where the lender agrees to take less (short) of the full mortgage amount." Where there is to be a short sale of a property, the lender must agree in writing in advance of the sale. Obviously, this is not a viable option if you want to keep the property because a short sale is just that: it is a sale. But if you are an investor wanting to get out from under a mountain of debt and you are not concerned about keeping the property, then the short sale may be an option for you.

The Straw Man Short Sale

The only possible way a short sale benefits a homeowner who wants to keep his property is if the homeowner finds a person to buy the property from the lender in a short sale and then agree to sell it to the homeowner for the same reduced price. Normally, this would not be a family member. Unfortunately, lenders will not make a short sale to a homeowner. Also, they will not normally make any significant mortgage reduction. However, they will reduce the mortgage when it is sold to a third person. Some of the reason for this is that the lender will not receive help from the government to cover a deficiency if the home is sold or the mortgage is reduced for the original borrower. However, if the property is sold to a third person, then the lender can collect some of the deficiency from the bailout funds. So, if the homeowner wants to buy the property with true mortgage principal reduction, it must be done through a third person. It's normal for the homeowner to pay some kind of a premium and cost to the third person for this kind of assistance. It is important to make certain that there is no fraud involved in the transaction. There should not be anything illegal about an arms-length arrangement that is fully disclosed.

One must remember that there can be tax consequences and mortgage deficiency consequences involved in any short sale. It is important to have good legal representation to make sure that any agreements signed with the lender include provisions that eliminate the possibility of any liability for a deficiency and also eliminate any liability for any future tax consequences for a mortgage deficiency. Some lenders may agree to this and some may not. It is more a factor of the particular lender's policies, and perhaps also a factor of the local market where the property is located. If a short sale can be arranged, then it is worth a try. Perhaps the most difficult part would be for the homeowner to be able to find financing to cash out the third party in a cash transaction. It can be done with hard-money lenders so long as the homeowner can show sufficient income to make the repayments. Often after successfully paying a high interest rate to a hard-money lender, one is able then to refinance for a more desirable lower interest rate after proving themselves (by paying on the new mortgage for a year or two.

A better possibility is to find a third-party investor willing to wait a year or two to receive their full funds reimbursed by a sale to the homeowner. In that case, a lease with an option to purchase can be negotiated between the third-party investor and the homeowner. With a successful history of making rental payments for a couple of years, the homeowner may be able to qualify for a regular mortgage and avoid having to use a hard-money lender.

In addition to a short sale opportunity, the investor can instead wait and purchase the property at a foreclosure auction for a possibly lower price. However, there is no assurance that the investor will prevail at the auction, so a short sale is normally the choice of preference. Also, there is the factor of the foreclosure remaining on the credit record of the homeowner. There are firms who make short sales available. Typically, they buy the home and then lease it back to the homeowner with an option to purchase the home within three years. The terms are not overbearing, and this can be an option for some people.

Solution 6. Tender of Payment

There is a rule of law that says if a debtor makes an offer (tender) of full complete payoff payment of all of a debt to a creditor, and the creditor refuses that payment, then the debt is fully satisfied. This is referred to as a "tender." Now we will discuss how the tender can work for you as a solution to your mortgage mess. This is actually quite an ingenious solution, and holds great promise as a viable way out of the mortgage mess. The tender works as follows.

First, it is important to determine precisely how much is owed to the lender. To accomplish this, simply contact the lender and ask for a payoff amount for the debt. It is a good idea to add some amount to the payoff total you are given, just to be sure to include any penalties, interest, or legal fees, or whatever else the lender may add to the debt at the last moment. So, if the outstanding mortgage balance is calculated as $225,000, then perhaps the tendered amount should be at least $230,000, just to be sure the full amount of debt is covered. This prevents the lender from challenging the tender later as being insufficient.

So after the tender amount is determined, then it is necessary to find an investor who will actually put up the tender amount into an escrow account. It is necessary to have the full tender amount available to be considered serious and valid by the lender. It is not enough to just say that one would like to pay off the debt. The funds must be real, available, and ready. So now we are in a position where the investor has put up money, and his money is at risk if the lender accepts the Tender. However, there is more to it than that. No investor in his or her right mind would put up $230,000 for a property that now may only be worth $100,000.

So to make this option a viable solution, there is some homework that must be accomplished first. One should have an audit done on the mortgage ownership. That would normally include both a forensic audit as well as a securitization audit. If one can demonstrate to the investor that the mortgage debt is, in fact, owned by someone other than the foreclosing lender, then there is a possible solution.

It is important that the tender be made with the condition that the lender, or pretender lender, must prove ownership of the debt. One would not want to pay a debt to some party who did not own the debt. If the lender cannot prove ownership of the debt, then they cannot lawfully accept the tender. That means the tender must be refused; and, of course, we know that if it is refused, then the debt is considered satisfied vis-à-vis that particular party, the pretender lender.

So even if the lender refuses the tender, they will not normally be so quick to cancel your debt. However, you can use the facts of these events, and then go to court and sue for a quiet title action against the lender, requesting relief from the court to grant summary judgment to have the court issue an order that can be recorded with the county recorder to remove any and all liens associated with this lender and this particular debt. This is not a solution that has been used much yet, but it is one that promises to hold great potential for many who are mired in the mortgage mess created by Wall Street.

Solution 7. Selective Short Refinance

A new potential solution has just begun to possibly become available for some select homeowners. This is what I term the "selective short refinance." This is a situation where the existing lender agrees to take a payoff for less than the amount of the outstanding debt. Normally, a lender will not short sell a home to the occupying homeowner. One reason is because they do not get as beneficial treatment on their taxes and bail-out payments from the government (which, remember, have been funded by the US tax-paying public). The reason lenders are reluctant to make loan modifications is similar.

However, in certain cases where these lenders have such little invested, it is possible to get a solution. For example, Chase paid only $1.9 billion for WaMu's assets that were worth over $310 billion. That means Chase paid only .0064 cents on the dollar. The single-family home loan portfolio was valued at $118 billion. It may be worth mentioning that Chase also got all of WaMu's branch banks thrown into the deal as well. Now, if Chase can foreclose on a property with a mortgage debt of $300,000 and a street fair-market value of only $150,000, what will they do? Even using all of the $1.9 billion as a cost basis, and using the $118 billion as a total, Chase only paid 1.6 cents on the dollar. That $300,000 mortgage only cost Chase $480. Remember, they will have lots of costs to pay real estate taxes, homeowners' association dues, maintenance, insurance, landscaping costs, and fix-up costs, in addition to the legal fees and real estate commissions and holding period fees. The most they may net after all that is maybe only $100,000.

Recently, it has come to the attention of many that it is quite possible that Chase did not in fact purchase the WAMU loan portfolio from the FDIC. Indications are that Chase only bought the branch banks, the deposits, and the loans that had already foreclosed. It appears that Chase did not purchase most of the loans that had not already foreclosed. This is a great defense in any action against Chase.

The homeowner can offer an alternative by getting an FHA-insured loan for 97 percent of the $150,000 value, which is $145,500. The lender has no legal costs nor any of the other costs associated with foreclosure. So, on an investment of $480 they can get $145,500, which leaves a profit of $145,020. The foreclosure profit would have been $100,000 less the $480 for a net result of $99,520. So, the selective short refinance solution nets the pretender lender $45,500 more in profit. It is also quicker and less trouble and less risk. In certain situations this may be a good solution.

There would be certain qualifying conditions for a homeowner to achieve this solution. This would apply only to owner occupied homes where the mortgage is upside down but current on all payments. Also, the homeowner would have to show some kind of hardship such as a loss of job or income, or health issues, etc.

Now why would a homeowner want to do this? The only reason would be to have a quick, inexpensive resolution to their situation. It is hard to put a price tag on resolution. Every case is different, and everyone's needs and desires are different. It may be that WAMU never owned the loan in the first place, and this could be litigated. Nonetheless, resolution in and of itself is valuable.

BLOOMBERG...The Silver Bullet, or is it the Golden Bazooka, or is it the Platinum Howitzer...?

One tool that has proven to be of great importance in ALL solutions is the Bloomberg Financial Search and Declaration. As well as other companies such as Reuters and others, it is Bloomberg, Inc. that makes available financial data on all investments such as stocks and bonds as well as mortgage backed securities. With the Bloomberg terminal one is actually able to find a specific mortgage note and its location and status within a particular pool of mortgage backed securities.

This information can show who currently owns a particular mortgage note and whether it has been paid off and what is the status of the note. This can virtually preempt the need for discovery and may allow a litigant to move directly into a motion for summary judgment with sanctions for the other side for bringing fraud upon the court as they try to refute the clear evidence of where and who owns the debt.

We had one case where the counsel for the lenders and servicers brought a one page "Affidavit of Ownership" relating to a mortgage note. This was a TRO hearing to ask the court to prevent the sale of the borrower plaintiff's home. So counsel for the other side gave a copy of their highly suspect affidavit to the judge and to our counsel. She thought she had the case won. Well because we had the clear evidence and also an expert witness in court ready to testify, our counsel was able to state unequivocally that her affidavit was a fraudulent document in contradiction of our clear evidence which was obtained using the Bloomberg Terminal and other research involving the 424B5 mortgage back securities Pooling and Servicing Agreement. It seemed as if the other counsel could "smell the sanctions in the air" for bringing fraud upon the court. The judge decided to continue the hearing for one week. The other attorney for the lenders and servicers grew pale as a sheet. She knew she did not want to come back in front of this judge again. She probably knew of the Massachusetts case where lenders and their respective attorneys were sanctioned $650,000 for bringing fraud into a bankruptcy court.

Without the information available from Bloomberg, one has to take the traditional route of litigation as an attorney. Typically it goes like this. The Borrower, who is the Plaintiff in a non-judicial state has to file a complaint. His attorney hopes he will survive a motion to dismiss by the other side so one can enter the second phase of litigation which is discovery. Even though one may be assured that his client has a good strong case, nonetheless, traditionally it can be difficult to find the evidence to prove the case. In discovery one can use the court to compel the production of documents and answers to interrogatories, hoping that the other side will play fair and not stonewall and hide pertinent facts.

However, by contrast with the information available on Bloomberg, one can have all the necessary information up-front even before the complaint is filed. With the information available on Bloomberg, we can prove who has the ownership of the debt. Fortunately, the debt cannot be in two places at once. Every attorney in the nation who is representing Borrowers needs to have access to this vital information on Bloomberg. This can be accomplished by subscribing to the Bloomberg service and acquiring the necessary training to use the terminal, or one can go to other providers such as can be found at **www.SolveMyMortgageMessNow.com**. Goldman Sachs has said publicly that they expect another 12 million foreclosures in the next few years. For every foreclosure there are probably 3 or 4 homes that are underwater financially. MERS purportedly is named on about 68 million mortgages in their system. So, this problem is not going to go away anytime soon. Some say that the foreclosure defense industry will become larger for attorneys than the personal injury industry. Time will tell. Nonetheless, there is a VERY large opportunity to render service and help to beleaguered homeowners with the information available through Bloomberg and a decent litigator attorney.

So as soon as the hearing was dismissed, this attorney made a beeline to remove her case to the Federal court. She did not want to reappear in front of this particular state judge with her highly suspect "affidavit of ownership." Later in Federal court the TRO was granted in favor of the borrower Plaintiffs.

We call this a Trust Search where we use Bloomberg software to go and actually find any particular mortgage note, where it is, who owns it, how many tranches it is in, and what its status is.

So the Bloomberg information is extremely valuable, and gives us a tremendous edge as we go into court. NO longer do we have to wait for the court to maybe compel the other side to divulge information that will work against them. Now we have that information up front and ready to go to win a case for the borrower.

The evidence from the Bloomberg Trust Search works equally well in both civil court as well as Bankruptcy court. It is almost impossible for a non-creditor to prove he is a creditor against the weight of the Trust search declaration and report. The note cannot be in two places at once. And again, to allege otherwise can run the risk of attorneys bringing fraud upon the court and possibly sanctions against them.

All attorneys looking to expand their business should consider the foreclosure defense opportunity available today. But as the saying goes, "Don't go to a gunfight with a knife!" Any attorney entering into the foreclosure defense field should seriously consider obtaining a subscription to the Bloomberg terminal and the training to properly operate it. This can be delegated to a paralegal or secretary easily enough. The rewards both financially and in terms of helping people are enormous.

To find out more about this silver bullet Trust Search, or use of our expert witnesses related to this subject, contact **www.SolveMyMortgageMessNow. com**. Often the fraudulent foreclosing servicers assert that they own or represent the owner of the debt. The data from the Bloomberg system can defeat them outright as it show the correct owner, and that the servicer has no interest in the note. This information can be used in conjunction with any of the strategies mentioned above. For more information on the Bloomberg Audit go to **www. SolveMyMortgageMessNow.com**

Solution Summary

We have now briefly examined seven solutions to help you get relief from this mortgage mess. No one solution will be the perfect solution for everyone because each person has their own particular set of priorities and particular needs. The seven solutions are: mediation, modification, litigation, debt relief, short sale, tender, and selective short refinance. Some of these solutions can actually be combined. For example, for a quick way to stop a foreclosure sale, one can file a Chapter 13 bankruptcy. This will gain time for the person to evaluate other solutions that may be a better fit in the long run. The Chapter 11 solution keeps the bankruptcy off of one's personal credit record, so it is a good option if that is a concern. Modification can be used as a means to gain more time if a sale is not already pending. Reading this material over more than once is a good exercise, and take notes about the pros and cons of each solution as it refers to your personal situation. This will help you find the right solution for yourself. Also, after you have gotten a decent understanding of the solutions, then you will want to speak with your own counselors and professional representatives. We will talk more about how to find good representation in the coming pages of this book. You can also read the blog affiliated with this book; created for homeowners and others to share their thoughts and ideas and experiences, it will hopefully serve as a means to support one another as a community in this fight to save America's family homes, one home at a time. The blog can be found at **www.SolveMyMortgageMessNow. com**. There, you will also find other resources to assist you in your own personal battle to defend your own castle from the invading dragons.

Help to Get a Handle on the Right Solution for YOU

So now with all this information, how does one process it so as to come up with an actual plan to move ahead? I realize there is more important information yet to come, but it will be helpful at this point to simply ask some questions about the different solutions, while they are fresh in your mind from just reading about them.

Before we look at the actual solutions themselves, it is important that we first speak about you, your family, and your relationships. Quite possibly, you and those close to you are in one of the most extremely stressful periods of your life so far. Hopefully, no one is bleeding yet; so there is still hope, right? Yes, of course. Later, we will discuss more about you and your family, but suffice it to say for now that your relationships are far more important than the house or anything else. We will cover some information further on to help in this regard, but for now just know that your relationships, including your own personal health, is more important than the house. Does that mean you should just walk away from your house? No. Probably this is not the solution. You may walk away from the house, but that does not mean you are walking away from the problem. Unfortunately, this problem has legs and has the ability to walk right behind you and follow you wherever you go.

Sit down with your family, and explain to them as much as you can what is going on. There is no substitute for communication. One cannot just keep one's head in the sand about this problem. It needs to be faced, and that is one of the main purposes of this book: to help you face and overcome this giant problem. David took out the giant Goliath in ancient times with only one smooth stone. Let's hope you can eventually put your giant problem away with this one relatively smooth book to help you. Tell your family that no matter what happens, your love and your relationships will remain strong and intact. Ask everyone to agree to be supportive of one another through this time. Tell them that better days will come in the future, but that right now everyone can choose to make the current days some of the best ever. It seems in life that often in times of struggle we rise to some of the best times ever, if we make that choice. We will speak more about coping and how to thrive in the midst of this awful situation later. Faith and prayer in these circumstances can actually be of great benefit to everyone and draw everyone closer together and stronger. If you don't know how to pray, it's easy. Just speak in a normal voice, describe the problem, ask for help, and say "amen" at the end. It's your choice to sit, stand or kneel. It can be that simple. Now let's get back to the solutions, and how to find the best one for you.

First, it is worth asking yourself (always also include your family, too) if you really want to fight to keep the house. It will be a fight, and that is okay. There are lots of fights in life, and this is one that is generally worth fighting. But on the other hand, you must ask if this is an opportunity to make a change that could include a move, either local or distant. This raises questions about schools, relatives, jobs, and lots of other things. However, you don't want to enter a fight and then start to wonder in the midst of the fight if you are doing the right thing. Get your decision made first, and then stick to it as a commitment. In this regard, it is helpful to evaluate what your other alternatives could be. Would you stay local and just rent a house? You always have to consider all of the costs involved? Remember, the cost of a move can equal the initial cost to begin a lawsuit against your lender. So if you have to spend money anyway, why not spend it on fighting to keep your home? This is a question you must answer as you go along. Don't expect to fully answer that question right at this moment. In addition to completing your own analysis, you also want to get the input of other professionals and then make your final decision. You can benefit from a situation evaluation by the staff of Go Free Network to see what may be the best solution for you at this time. See the

Resource Guide at the end of the book, or their website, for more information on this service.

Another question to ask is: how much time do you have? Do you already have a notice of default (sent to you from your servicer of your mortgage)? Do you already have a sale date sent to you (as a "notice of sale")? The amount of time you either have or do not have will give impact to shape your decision, in part. Remember, some activities like mediation and modification can gain you more time.

An important question to ask is: how much money do you have available to spend on your solution? Are you and your spouse (if you are married) both still gainfully employed? Are you able to save money for a housekeeping fund at this time? If you are not currently making mortgage payments, then hopefully you will be able to fund the rescue of your home from the clutches of the evil dragon of greed who made his home on Wall Street and breathed fire all across America. You will want to budget for your solution, whichever you choose, both in time and money.

You should ask yourself if a form of debt relief is appropriate for you. Can you qualify for a Chapter 7, or Chapter 13, or Chapter 11 in the bankruptcy courts? Is your income too low or too high? Is your debt too high? Do you have lots of other assets that you do not want to give up to satisfy creditors? Do you have a lot of debt other than your home mortgages? Does your job require a security clearance that may be affected by a bankruptcy on your credit record?

Do you know anyone who would have enough funds available either in cash or in borrowed funds such that a short sale could be accomplished? Or, do you have enough cash so that a tender could be attempted? Do you think that someone would be willing to help you? Is it worth asking them now to get a preliminary indication of their openness and ability?

You may want to consider having a forensic audit and/or a securitization audit performed on your mortgage loan to determine what possibilities may be available to you in terms of causes of action to allege against your lender. You may also want to determine how difficult it may be for your lender to prove or not prove ownership of your mortgage debt. You may want to send a qualified written request to your lender to establish some of the foundation for further actions to be taken at a later date.

As you begin to interview attorneys and other professionals, begin to assemble a team to help you fight to keep your home and solve your mortgage mess. We will speak about how to identify and choose your team members in a later chapter.

If you are going to consider litigation, then you will want to go to the following website to learn what a lawsuit is all about. The website is as follows: www.jurisdictionary.com?refercode=CC0008

The author receives a small referral fee, but your cost is the same no matter whether you buy direct or otherwise. For a relatively small fee you can get a very good education about what a lawsuit is all about. You will also receive forms that can be used as templates. I cannot recommend that you represent yourself, and you will remember the old saying, "He who represents himself has a fool for a lawyer." Nonetheless, for less than you would pay an attorney for one hour, you can learn a lot of valuable information about how the courts work, and what actually happens in a lawsuit. This will indeed enable you to make a better choice about who to hire, and how to manage your attorney. Remember he is working for you. So you must know a least a little about what he is supposed to be doing on your behalf. Suffice it to say this is a good investment in the overall picture.

Remember, recovery starts NOW, and it is your choice to manage the situation, and not let the situation abuse you and your loved ones any longer. Yes, recovery starts in your thoughts, and in your spoken words, and later on in your attitude and in your emotions. As you envision a solution to your situation it will become manifest as time goes on. The journey will not be without bumps and jerks, but it can lead to a good outcome for you. You will have to be strong throughout the process, and that is something no one else can do for you. Rest assured, you have everything you need to stay strong and complete the journey and arrive victorious.

CHAPTER FIVE

Find the Right People to Help

Obtaining the assistance of the right people to help you in the fight to keep your home and solve your mortgage mess is vital, essential, and important. Most of us do not have excess funds sufficient to try different professionals, so we need to get the decision correct the first time. Then, too, an unfortunate result the first time around may turn out to be the final result with no opportunity to try again. However, not to worry, this book will assist you and make choosing the right people easier.

You can benefit from educators in foreclosure defense, case evaluators, forensic mortgage auditors, securitization mortgage auditors, qualified attorney referrers, professional experienced attorneys, understanding case managers, expert witnesses, and others, depending upon your circumstances. See the Resource Guide and the Exhibits at the end of the book and the website for more information on these services.

So let's start with education. First, you need to have some understanding of what is going on and how it came to be if you are going to solve your mortgage mess. As has been said, first identify the problem so that you can then solve the problem. You have made a good choice by purchasing this book so you can get some understanding of exactly how we have arrived at our current location. There are not many other books yet that deal with this subject. However, there are many websites and articles that can help you understand what is really going on, how it happened, and how to move on from here to get free of the situation. See the Resource Guide at the end of the book for more information on education. Remember, only YOU can take responsibility for getting out of this mess. No one will do it for you, but YOU can get it done. So, just stop, take a deep breath, and forge on.

Now, even after you have educated yourself, you still have to ask yourself if you really understand everything that is going on and whether or not you are able to know which solution is best for you. This is where you will benefit from meeting with a qualified person with experience, even if just by telephone, to discuss your situation, ask (the right) questions, understand where you are, and discuss the different solution options as well as how they may apply to you. It is a long journey to get free, and it is worth it. However, it is very important to begin on the right road, and the best road, to get the best result in the best amount of time with the most cost-effective dollars invested.

You may want to consider having a forensic mortgage audit performed on your behalf to determine the most flagrant violations that occurred in the creation and the servicing of your loan. This can be ammunition for you to use later in your fight to win your property. Depending if you end up in federal court or state court, these violations can produce damage awards that can help cover the cost of a portion of your expenses for the fight. Again, the more you understand just how you were wronged, the more resolute and determined you will be in fighting to recapture and keep your property.

A sibling to the forensic mortgage audit is the mortgage securitization audit. The securitization audit does not focus so much on the violations of federal and state statutory laws; the securitization audit focuses more on following the ownership trail of your mortgage note to determine who, if anyone, has any rights associated with your mortgage note and your deed of trust. This is a very involved research project that can take many hours to complete, requiring a search through millions of mortgage records to find just one mortgage note—yours—among so many millions of others. However, once found, this information is crucial to bringing overwhelming evidence to the court in your fight as to who has rights and who does not have any rights related to your property. This is one of the most important pieces of ammunition you can bring into the fight to solve your mortgage mess and shed the light of truth upon what really transpired after you signed the loan documents at your mortgage closing.

One of the biggest decisions you will have to make is which attorney to work with. While some people have filed lawsuits themselves, it is very complicated to truly conduct a lawsuit without any experience. In the few cases where "pro se" or "in proper person" plaintiffs have been able to prevail by litigating their own cases there was usually some very flagrant, obvious fraud, such as forged signatures, etc. This kind of case can be won. However, where the allegations are subtler, it becomes more difficult. Here is an analogy for you. Your three-year-old child needs a brain surgery. Someone gives you a knife. Okay, now where do you cut? In other words, just because you have a knife, and a desire for your child to be well, that still does not make you a qualified brain surgeon. Typically, the pretender lenders hire the best and the biggest of the attorneys to represent them. So one has to go into the court and go against some of the toughest seasoned opponents who know all the procedural tricks to dance circles around you. Also, most judges do not have much sympathy for pro se litigants. All the judges have overloaded dockets, and they don't have much patience for individuals who really don't understand how to conduct a lawsuit.

So how do you find a good attorney? How do you distinguish a good attorney from a mediocre one, or sometimes a bad one? The saying goes that a good attorney knows the law, and a great attorney knows the judge. There is some truth to that statement, but even so there is much more to a great attorney than just perhaps knowing the judge. We will suggest some ways for you to determine how to select a good attorney a little later on. But for now, I want to mention a few other professionals that you may also want to call on to assist you as part of your team.

It helps to have a "case manager;" you might think of this person as a coach who can assist you as the fight continues. This person will not only listen to your questions and find answers, but will also be available to communicate with you on a regular basis, to keep you informed with what is happening with your case, what the timetable is, and what to expect. Most attorneys cannot give this kind of time to a client. They are busy drafting, doing research, attending hearings, directing discovery, and other aspects of the lawsuit. The case coach can be a go-between for you and your attorney. This doesn't mean that you never talk with the attorney. But generally, you will want an update more frequently than the attorney can give. Remember, one definition of a lawsuit is "hurry up and wait." It is during the long waiting periods that having a knowledgeable, informed person to speak with is helpful.

Other team members may include expert witnesses. Where do you find credible, qualified expert witnesses, and for which aspect of your case do you need to enlist them? You may also want to speak with a counselor at some time during your case. How do you find a good counselor versus one who takes your money and is not helpful?

At **www.SolveMyMortgageMessNow.com**, you can find good, experienced and qualified personnel to help you as members of your team to solve your mortgage mess. Also, see our list of services in the Resource Guide at the end of this book. Remember, this is ultimately about not just your property, but about your life. So it is important to identify the best help available to you. It is too traumatic and stressful to have one problem with your mortgage, and then have a second problem with your attorney who is supposed to be helping you—not making problems and putting you further in debt.

Finding the Right Attorney

There are a variety of approaches to finding the right attorney. One can do everything from reading the local *Yellow Pages* ads to searching the *Martindale Hubble* attorney directory, and everything in between. You can speak with friends to ask for referrals. However, you must recall that this particular niche of law has never been taught in law school. The seeds of this mortgage meltdown were only sowed less than ten years ago, and the market did not truly crash until 2008. So, this is a whole new field of law in which most attorneys have little or no experience. Even if an attorney has twenty or thirty years of experience, it is likely they have never handled a wrongful foreclosure case. What are the arguments? What are the weak points of the lenders? What are the best causes of action to allege in any one particular case? How can all the cases be similar, and yet at the same time each case is particular?

One can talk to others to gain opinions and insights, but one must remain vigilant not to be overly influenced by someone who is not really qualified to give an opinion. Talk and listen, but keep your own opinion and judgment guarded. Generally, you will know when you are getting good advice, and when you are not, or when the advice is questionable. Trust your inner self to recognize the difference.

The type of attorney you are looking for will be determined somewhat by the solution you are seeking. Are you going to litigate, or are you going to file a Chapter 13 bankruptcy? Perhaps you need to talk to one or more or each type of attorney before you make up your mind. Usually, most attorneys do not charge for the initial consultation. Do not let yourself be "sold" on any one solution just because it is the specialty of the attorney you are speaking with. I would always tell the attorney you will get back to him. Thank them for their time, and then retreat to make your decision on your own.

Here is a list of questions you can ask an attorney:
1. How long have you been in practice?
2. What areas do you specialize in?
3. How much litigation experience do you have?

4. How many jury trials have you conducted?

5. What is your record of results?

6. Do you also handle bankruptcies, or just litigation?

7. Have you done any foreclosure defense work yet?

8. What is your opinion on the current mortgage crisis and how it came about? (Look for any bias here, toward the lender or the borrower. Does this attorney favor the consumer or does he favor big business?)

9. Are you open to new ideas on legal theory?

10. What is your opinion on the position of most of the local judges on the mortgage crisis? Are they pro lender or pro borrower?

11. Who are some of your current clients?

12. Do you represent any lenders or banks? (He may have a conflict of interest.)

13. What is your hourly rate?

14. Do you ever work on a contingency or success fee?

15. Will you consider a combination fee that includes something now and something later on based on a contingency?

16. What do you think is a decent budget for a litigated case?

17. How many of your cases are settled before they go to court?

18. What kind of settlements have you been able to achieve?

19. Could you provide any referrals of current or past clients?

20. Do you have any complaints from the Bar against you now?

21. Have you ever been sued for malpractice?

22. If you will not take my case for whatever reason, will you recommend some other attorneys?

23. Do you know of any potential expert witnesses, mortgage auditors, or securitization auditors?

24. How busy are you? Do you have time for my case?

Now that you have seen this list of questions, you must understand and appreciate the answers almost like reading between the lines. Even if you have all the answers, it can still be difficult to truly appreciate the answers in a manner that will lead you to make a good choice in determining who to select for your legal representation. Again, *Solve My Mortgage Mess Now!* will assist you with this important decision (see the Resource Guide for more information on this service, regardless of where you are located). Sometimes it is necessary to actually train the attorney in foreclosure defense, if there is no one in a given area who is qualified to take on your case. This is possible also. We have done this in the past in different jurisdictions and different states, and it can be repeated as is necessary.

I don't recommend you attempt to represent yourself in court. But I do recommend that you go to **www.SolveMyMortgageMessNow.com** and select the link to www.jurisdictionary.com?refercode=CC0008 under "Links." There you will find a company that will supply you with commonly used legal forms. This will give you a great basic education that will allow you to work better and smarter with your attorney. The cost is less than one hour of attorney time and well worth it in savings than can be generated.

We have spoken about how this mortgage mess came about, what is happening as a result of it, what some of the solutions can be, and how to identify the right people to help. Now it is time for us to speak more directly about how you are doing in the midst of it all. It is important that you are able to not only save your home but also save your life and the life of your family and loved ones in the middle of all the stress and turmoil that is swirling around in our economy and our society today. In the next chapter we want to address the best practices to cope with this temporary situation and how to best recover from it in a way that you can benefit and thrive, not just survive.

PART THREE

How to Cope and Recover

CHAPTER SIX

Best Coping Mechanisms

So HERE WE ARE. Now what? This is probably the most important chapter in the book. Everything else in the book is about your house. This chapter is about YOU! Always remember, YOU are more important than your house. Your house is important, but you are more than your house, and your house does not define you. There is a greater reality about you that is deeper and more significant than the roof over your head. Simply put, your head is more valuable than the roof over it! So now let's get into it. I encourage you to put aside all preconceptions and keep an open mind throughout this discussion. Swallow the fish, and spit out the bones. Keep what works for you now, and consider coming back later and taking a second look. This chapter is one of those chapters worth reading again and again. Different techniques and different aspects of those techniques will speak to you in different ways over time and as circumstances change and develop. Some things need time to be pondered after being read for some length of time. Some things will need to be tried and experimented with to see what works well. So with these words we will now talk about how to cope and how to recover.

In one sense, coping and recovery go together. Different time periods are involved, but there is just one YOU to continue on through both periods. Some of the thoughts and ideas shared regarding coping will also apply to recovery and vice versa.

As someone has said, "You are the sum of your thoughts." In the Book of Proverbs it says, "As a person thinks, so are they." As we are going to learn, thoughts are very important in both coping and recovery. We must understand that we are free to choose which thoughts we think. Depending upon which thoughts we think, this can have a large influence on how we experience life and what the results of life are for us. Thoughts are somewhat like birds in this analogy. We think of our mind as a tree, and we think of different thoughts as birds. We may not be able to keep different thoughts from landing on a particular branch of our tree, but we can certainly keep them from staying there and building a nest and hatching and raising an entire flock of similar birds. We are free to shoo away the birds and the thoughts that we do not want to have in our tree. Generally, we don't want negative, fearful thoughts building nests and dominating our thought life. We want positive, faith-filled thoughts to occupy our thought life. We must remember that we are free to choose which thoughts fill our mind, and as we think so shall we be.

Let's give an example of how this analogy can be applied in our situation. Let's say we are a few months behind on our mortgage payments, and we are not sure if we should continue to make any more payments or not. Here we have a choice. Do we dwell on the possibility of the sheriff knocking on our door in the middle of the night and putting us out on the street with no notice? If we think like that we will be in an almost constant state of panic and fear, completely stressed out, and not much good to ourselves or anyone else. Remember, the choice is yours. It is better to choose to think we have solutions available to us. We are going to acquire the help we need to make a good decision and reach a good result concerning our living situation. If we choose to think this way, speak this way, and eventually believe this way, we will be much happier, more loving, and a better person to those who are close to us at home and at work. The choice is ours. Someone has said that the definition of worry is "prayer in reverse." Well, I don't know about that, but I do know that worry certainly does not help anything, and it can make us worse. It can even damage our physical health, our relationships, and our productivity.

We need to discover the truth about our situation and base our thought on the truth. We have all heard the expression, "You shall know the truth, and the truth shall make you free." So if we want to be free, we need to learn the truth and then keep our thoughts on things that are true. The truth is not always just what we see and just what we hear. Often there is a deeper truth that can be known, but cannot necessarily be seen or heard. It is that truth that we are looking for. This is truth that we more often recognize in our spirit than in our mind. Once we recognize it, then we can direct our mind to it, and keep our mind there. There is a part of us that is deeper than just our thoughts. It is our spirit, and the spirit can manage the thought life. It may take some practice at first, but it can be done. Maybe we need to spend some quiet time away from all the hustle and bustle and TV and other stimuli. When we get quiet, we have a better chance of recognizing the truth in that instant or even later in the midst of a lot of activity. In the latter, it was the time spent in quiet that primed us to recognize the truth later. This is not a religious book, so I am not going to talk a lot more at this point about spiritual things. However, I will say this regarding my personal opinion. I suppose there are about five major religions. Those would be Hinduism, Buddhism, Islam, Judaism, and Christianity. Jesus Christ was a Jewish rabbi, so one can say he incorporates two out of five, or about forty percent. Then he goes on to say, "Ask anything in my name and it will be done for you." He also says, "If two of you on earth agree about anything, it will be done for you." He makes other such statements about the faith the size of a grain of mustard seed being able to move mountains, etc., (like a mountain of debt, for instance). So from my perspective, He offers the best deal out there, and so I lean heavily in His direction from simply practical perspectives. I do know that God cares for you and he wants to help you in your current situation. You will have to make up your own mind about how you want to believe and pray, etc. I will write another book to talk more about these things. That will come about sometime next year. For now, we want to stay focused on solving the mortgage mess; and in this chapter, right now, we want to stay focused on learning how to cope and recover.

Coping with the Mortgage Mess

Let's focus on the best coping practices. First, you want to educate yourself. We have already spoken about that, and you have taken a great first step in reading this book. Other resources are listed in the Resource Guide in the back of the book, and they will also help you.

Very important: You should not accept, but you should refuse, any thought or feelings of guilt or self-condemnation. You did not create this situation you are in. In fact, you were lured into this situation because other people wanted to make large sums of money off of your actions without you being aware of it. This is like the pickpocket who wants to steal your wallet without your knowing about it. If the pickpocket gave full disclosure before he acted, no one, or at least very few people, would ever lose their wallet. Typically, it is not the victim of the pickpocket who is responsible for the injury done to them. It was the pickpocket who did the wrong. So don't feel guilty about your situation. Let's get your situation solved, and allow you to move on with the rest of your life, which is waiting for you now.

Next it is necessary to seek help, and also to pray. Start wherever you are. Doing nothing is your worst enemy. Having your own private or public pity party is the closest cousin of Doing Nothing. However, I realize you do need to express your grief, your concern, your disappointment, your frustration, your anger, and whatever else you are experiencing. But do this in a way that does not injure anyone else or yourself. Go out to the fields, or the desert, or the mountains, or your closet and scream your head off if you need to. But once you have done it, then it is over. Now it is time to get busy with the job, and, yes, it is a job to solve your mortgage mess. Think of it as a job, and treat it as a responsibility. Hey, you are still alive, you are still breathing, and you are not bleeding blood, even though we have all bled a lot of cash over the past ten years.

Also very important: Be sure you talk with your children to enlighten them and protect them during this time of intense stress and unsettling events. Depending upon their age, go ahead and share with them the cause of all this mortgage mess. Include your children with you in terms of being positive, praying for good results, and the other things that will be covered in this chapter.

Brainstorm about how you can give to others. This may be to family members, relatives, neighbors, strangers, the homeless, or whoever. You can give time, money, service, advice, entertainment, or whatever you have in your quiver of possible contributions to make to other people. There is a principle that says, "Give and it shall be given to you." You can put that principle into motion by being the one to start it. Sometimes people speak of this as "paying it forward." If you want something good to happen for you, then start doing good things for other people. Sow the seeds of goodness and good actions, and just like in the plant world you will always reap what you sow.

Guard your relationships. Don't be overwhelmed by the fog of stress, pain, doubt, fear, and whatever else is happening. Know that all of that is just like a fog that rolled in on the coast. It is hard to see in the fog. But don't worry. The fog will lift, and the sun will break through. You will be able to see clearly again. So even if for now you must act on instinct instead of vision, that is okay. Remember, this current situation is only temporary, and your relationships can be permanent. Don't give up something permanent and valuable just because of some temporary painful experience. Be tough and do whatever you need to stick together and fight through to the other side of this mortgage mess. What am I speaking about? Well, financial stress is one of the prime causes of divorce. Don't let the crooks on Wall Street wreck your family as well as your finances. You can solve the financial mess. So just make sure that you care for each other through it all. Do you know that divorced couples increase the odds that their children will also divorce by

80 percent? You don't want to pass that heritage on to your children. So hang in there. Better days are coming. Seek out the help you need and find a way to work through things together.

It is important to make an agreement together to stay positive. This starts with your thoughts, but it also includes your speech and your actions as well. We all make mistakes, so be forgiving of each other. If we slip up and get negative in some way, whether in speech or action toward others, or whatever, hey, just apologize, say you're sorry, and get back on the positive wagon. It's not that big of a deal. It's nothing more than a speed bump on the highway to solving your mortgage mess. So get over it, and keep moving in a positive direction.

Now this is where your faith can grow. That is a good thing. It is good to have lots of faith. What am I talking about? Well, I suggest that you start believing in some miracles to help you get out of this situation that you are in. You may experience a miracle and you may not. I cannot say. But either way, you will be better off for having faith and believing for some miracles to happen. I know one couple that has not made a mortgage payment in two years, and they are still in their home and no foreclosure has been started against them. I know another lady who is a single parent who has not made a payment in over two years, and no foreclosure was started against her. Finally, a foreclosure was started. Her attorney filed a lawsuit to stop the foreclosure. The foreclosure was stopped. But then it looked like the foreclosing trustee was going to come after her again. Next thing we know, the foreclosing trustee dismissed all legal proceedings against her. How does one explain these things? Well there may be some natural answers, but it is almost easier to think of these results as miracles. Call it what you like. The people are still in their homes. There are many other stories I could tell as well. The point is this: Miracles do happen, and you may as well be open to them. Let's solve your mortgage mess by any means possible. Bottom line is bottom line. So if we are going to believe in miracles, that means it is okay, permissible, and appropriate to ask for a miracle. Go for it, and be sure to tell me about it when it occurs. You can enter your story on the blog, which is found at **www.SolveMyMortgageMessNow.com.**

Manage your telephone: This is one very practical thing you can do to keep peace in your home. Use caller ID and/or become familiar with the phone numbers that are used by the dunning phone callers who work for your pretender lender. You have to understand that most of these people are not sophisticated. Most of them are paid a minimum wage plus a percentage of whatever they can twist your arm to send in. It is simply not worth talking to these people because, inevitably, they will ruin your day, try to make you feel guilty, speak demeaning to you, and do anything they can to make you feel bad. It is better to just simply not answer the phone. Enough said.

Now, there is one exception to this normal guideline of not answering. If you are working on a loan modification and the home retention department is calling you, then you may need to speak with them. Again, you can always let the call go to voice mail, and then just call them back. Or better yet, try to arrange it so that they communicate with you by email. It is a lot less intrusive, and a lot less emotionally charged. The point is you want to keep your peace. So do what you need to do to manage your phone so that *you* are in control, not the nagging collections-type people who are not respectful to you.

Without saying it just so, it goes without comment that you really do not need to panic over any of this. Again, people are not coming after you with guns drawn and blazing with bullets. It is not fun, but you can get through it and you will. There is never any reason to panic. So just relax, take a deep breath, realize that this is going to work out, and live from a place of peace in your life.

One piece of advice that will help you greatly is to remember to keep your sense of humor. Yes, you can actually laugh at your situation, and laugh with all the millions of others that are going through the exact same things that you are going through. It is okay to crack jokes about it all. You probably recall that the derivation of the word "mortgage" comes from the French, and the literal definition is to "shake hands with death." *Mort* is French for "death," and *gage* can be translated as a "handshake." Well, the mortgage is dead, and you are still alive, so go ahead and laugh at the mortgage situation. Laughter is actually very healthy, and when you can laugh at your own situation it is a good sign that you are on the road to a good solution.

You have to constantly keep things in perspective, that your life is much, much more than just the house where you live. Hard times come upon almost everyone at some point. People survive, and life goes on. Think of the people in Poland and Germany during and after World War II. They really had it bad, and they got through it. You are going to get through this, too.

Be sure to be putting money aside each month for your housing legal defense fund. You may not be paying your mortgage right now, but you should not be spending that money as if it is surplus. Be diligent. Live on a budget, and make sure you save for the execution of the solution that is right for you.

You can actually make this entire occurrence something of an adventure. Think of it however it best works for you. Think of it as a puzzle-solving exercise.

Imagine yourself on a reality TV show, and you have to find and execute the right solution for you to solve your mortgage mess. And, yes, there is a big prize waiting for you on the other side as the winner. The prize is that you will be out of the mortgage mess.

You may want to keep a diary of everything that happens. You definitely want to keep a written record of any and all conversations with your lender and/or servicer of your loan, especially if you are in a mortgage modification program where you have made an application and you are waiting for an answer. For example, if the lender tells you that you must miss two months mortgage payments to qualify for a modification. This may be helpful for you later if you file a lawsuit against your lender. These kinds of things are useful before a judge.

In addition to just taking notes on everything, you may want to write an article, or you may want to write a book about your experience. Having notes about all the details can preserve the options for you no matter what you may choose to do in the future. If nothing else, when it is all over, you can read the notes and have a good laugh about the whole episode with those who are close to you.

You may want to consider starting a mortgage mess support group. If you meet regularly, you can each share your experiences and what you have learned since the last meeting. One meeting about every two weeks is a pretty good rhythm. It is most helpful for new people to come to such a group to experience some support, gain some education, and realize they are not alone. This is a genuine service to the community. The group should have leadership, and should not just turn into a pity party. The focus should be one that is positive in nature and solution-oriented.

You may want to start a blog or website as a means of extending the reach of your support group. There is a way to turn lemons into lemonade. Each one just has to find their particular niche and how to go about it.

Remember, you can cope with all this, and you can stay on top of it all rather than being underneath it all. From a coping perspective you can grow into a posture of flourishing; you will get your coping legs under you and continue to grow in the practices outlined in this chapter. It is also a great time to foster personal growth, and a great time to be able to give to other people. It is in the crucible of challenge that we find our best selves. So go for it. You can do it, and you will never regret it.

Now we are going to move on from coping and flourishing to get into how you can recover. Remember that a lot of your recovery begins right now as you enter into the proper coping practices that will lead you into the best recovery.

CHAPTER SEVEN

Best Practices for a Healthy Recovery

MANY TIMES IT IS BEST to see the finished product from the beginning. So create in your mind a picture of what everything will look like, how your relationships will be, how you will enjoy being with those you love, and how life will be when all this is over and your mortgage mess is solved. Seriously, take some time, go and be quiet, and create a mental picture of all that was just mentioned above. Now, as you picture those things, go ahead and release your emotions and begin to feel just what it will feel like when you arrive at that destination. The process is a journey, and that power of that vision will empower you to do what is required to get there. Create a few sentences that describe the picture you have created, and then say those sentences out loud over and over again each day. This will give you strength, and will give you tenacity, and will keep you from giving in to discouragement.

Assuming you have protected your relationships well throughout the solution to your mortgage mess, you will have a joyful celebration when the solution brings the result you desire. This is the wisest investment you will make to keep your family intact. Then you will realize that, indeed, your family is much more valuable than your house, or any house, or even a palace.

In the future, you want to avoid debt. Remember in the old days, before credit, when department stores had "layaway" departments? People would make purchases and each week they would make a payment on the article until it was all paid for. Then they would receive it and have possession after it was paid for, and there was no interest charged. You can do that on your own. It is called saving! Just delay your gratification, and save up for whatever it is you want to purchase, and then pay for it with cash. It is a great feeling. And if you don't have the cash to pay for it, then that means you can't afford it. Just because you can borrow and pay for it with credit does not mean that you can afford it, at least not right now. Become a saver instead of a spender. The new successful symbol is no longer a large house with a pool and two luxury cars in the driveway with debt and interest payments beyond your eyeballs; no, the new success symbol is to be debt-free. Remember, debt-free means stress-free. You are no longer sharing your house with the banker and your car with the finance company. It sounds tough, but you can do it. Many other cultures have done it and many still do. So you can do it, too.

To accomplish this you will want to create a budget and also a financial plan. There are lots of materials and books that teach how to do both of those, so I am not going to cover that in any detail in this book. But, it is important. If you do not plan to succeed, then you are planning to fail. Or said another way, to fail to plan is to plan to fail. A few words, but they have so much meaning. Make it a core value in your household to refuse debt no matter how easy or how attractive it may appear to be. Consider ways to increase your income. Think of things you can do. You'll be surprised at all the possibilities that exist. Open up savings accounts in your bank. Deposit into them regularly. It will feel great. There are lots of good books and systems for getting out of debt. Check them out, and then get started with a good plan.

One of the best ways you can expect more is by giving more. Malachi, the prophet of ancient times, said that if we tithe to God, He opens the windows of heaven and pours out such a blessing upon us that we cannot contain it all. There are many other special readings about the practice of giving and how it can lead to much blessing in one's life. Make this a research project to learn more about this topic. You won't regret it.

One way to give in addition to giving money is to educate others about what you have learned. In addition to educating them, you can actually help them in whatever ways they need help. Continue to believe in yourself, believe in others, and do your best to make the world a better place for everyone. Think globally, but act locally. That's not a bad expression, especially the "act locally" part. If we just think about all the problems in the world at large, sometimes it can be overwhelming. Investigate what you can do in your own neighborhood to help someone and make their life just a little better. Even something as simple as being kind to other people can make a great difference to someone else, and it will bring a blessing to your life as well. It is true that it is more blessed to give than it is to receive. It is hard to understand that until a person actually does it. The understanding comes with the experience and the performance.

Resist judging others, and don't condemn yourself or anyone else. We all need each other in the end, so let's pull together to make everything just a little better for everyone else. We can be as innocent as doves and as wise as serpents at the same time. But now we want to use our wisdom for the right purposes, and not just for selfish on self-centered projects that don't really benefit others.

Epilogue

So what happened to our friends that we met in the beginning of the book? Remember Bob and Mary Jones, Jose and Maria Gonzales, and Paul and Gina Schwartz? Well, there is good news to report in each instance, for each couple. After separating briefly, and before their divorce was finalized, Bob and Mary had a chance to get together and talk about things and find some help. One of Mary's friends told her about a law firm that was doing some pro bono work to help distressed homeowners who had lost their homes in foreclosure. Since less than ninety days had expired since the unlawful foreclosure auction sale, Bob and Mary were able to join a large multi-plaintiff case, with the same lender being sued by many different borrowing homeowners, for little or no money. A temporary restraining order was approved by the court and stopped the eviction, and the Joneses were able to move back into their home before it was sold to any third party. Their case is still in litigation, but it is looking very favorable with new evidence that the lender did not actually own the debt. Their two children, Jenny and Johnny, are happy to be back in their home, attending the same school and getting on with life as usual. Bob and Mary admit that it was a really rough time for awhile, but now they say that the struggle they went through together has actually made their marriage stronger and their love for each other deeper. Bob recently found a new job, and their life is on the upswing in every way.

Jose and Maria Gonzales learned by attending a seminar that they could legally challenge their mortgage lender and put pressure on them through discovery in a lawsuit where the lender must prove they own the debt. The lender came back to them before the lawsuit was finished and offered to adjust their mortgage debt down to 90 percent of current market value. Jose and Maria were pleased, and agreed to accept the terms of the lender to adjust their mortgage. Now they are refocused on their dental careers, and they no longer spend hours worrying about what to do with their house.

Paul and Gina Schwartz decided to transfer all their rental properties each into its own separate limited liability company. Then the Schwartzes proceeded to bankrupt each of the LLCs in a Chapter 11 bankruptcy filing that had no impact upon their personal credit scores. In each of the bankruptcy filings the Schwartzes have disputed the ownership of the debt on each of the properties. Nine of their properties have been shown to not have any provable debt associated with them. The other eleven properties are still in the pipeline, waiting for hearing dates and more challenges. Things are looking very promising for all except two of the properties that have mortgages on them from a local credit union, which was not involved in the securitization business with the Wall Street companies.

Now What About YOU?

And, what will be the results of your situation? Will your mortgage mess be solved as well as the three couples listed above? I hope so. I hope you have gotten something out of this book to help you solve your own mortgage mess. Let me know how I can be of assistance to you. Be sure to examine the Resource Guide at the end of the book. There is a list of services there that may be very valuable to you in your own solution of your mortgage mess.

I will have a new book out in 2011 that will talk more about the spirit and how to tap into that provision to empower your life, to live better and better and stronger and stronger. I hope you will look for it, and benefit from it also. I want to thank you for allowing me to share my thoughts and my experience with you, and I hope you will pass it on to others.

I wish you all the very best, and may God bless you richly! It is He who said, "Owe no one anything but to love one another." Together let's live debt-free and get out of the mortgage mess forever! See you in the next book! **Le Fin.**

©2011 Charles W. Christmas, Jr., Esq., CMA, SMA

Exhibits

List of Exhibits

Exhibit A: Long-Form Qualified Written Request and Debt Validation

Exhibit B: Short-Form Qualified Written Request and Debt Validation

Exhibit C: Certified Authorization of Borrower

Exhibit D: Mortgage Review and Analysis Intake Form

Exhibit E: Arguments for Temporary Restraining Order and/or Preliminary Injunction

Exhibit F: Securitization Overview

Exhibit G: Simple Legal Statements and Questions That Need Answers

Exhibit H: Established Understanding of Notes and Mortgages/Deeds of Trust

Exhibit I: Congressional Testimony of Professor Adam Levitin, Esq.

Exhibit J: Bloomberg Securitization Audit Intake Form

Exhibit A
Long-Form Qualified Written Request and Debt Validation

Date:
YOUR NAME
STREET ADDRESS [of subject property]
CITY, STATE, ZIP CODE

NAME OF SERVICER
Attention: Debt Validation
STREET ADDRESS
CITY, STATE ZIP CODE   [sent via certified mail]
RE: LOAN NUMBER:

Dear SERVICER,

I am writing to challenge the validity of the debt on my home at [STREET ADDRESS], [STATE]. As you know there has been a lot in the news about the securitization of mortgage notes, and how the money was funded from New York security firms, rather than the presumed lender who was performing a service for a fee as a middleman in the mortgage process.

Please acknowledge this request within five (5) days and provide answers and corrections within thirty (30) days.

I need to receive from you evidence that you or the parties you represent actually are the holders in due course of any obligation that may have been created by me. A copy of the original is not sufficient since that note may have been sold numerous times. I need the information that shows the continuous chain of title without any gaps in time of the note, the recording of any assignments, and the authority of anyone who may have executed such assignments. I also request who is the current holder in due course of my alleged note, and where that obligation, if any, is physically being maintained and safeguarded.

In this day of AIG insurance payments, credit default swaps, and troubled assets relief programs, and other bail-out payments, I need to see a full accounting of my alleged note to see what, if any, payments have been applied to my alleged note.

This accounting falls under the auspices of the Qualified Written Request, as prescribed by Title 12 Section 2605 (e) of the United States Code as well as the Truth In Lending Act found at 15 U.S.C. Section 1601. I need to know what has happened to my alleged obligation.

I also want to see any Pooling and Servicing Agreements related to my alleged note and deed of trust as well as any Deposit Agreement, Servicing Agreements, Custodial Agreements, Master Purchase Agreements, Issuer Agreement, Commitments to Guarantee, and Any Trustee Agreements. I also need to see the Custodial Accounting related to the alleged note.

I need to see all copies of any Assignments of my alleged obligation, as well as any Electronic Transfers.

I need to see copies of any official county recordings of any documents related to my alleged obligation, and also any electronic recordings of all documents related to my alleged obligation.

I need to know who is the current holder in due course of my alleged obligation.

I need to see a copy of your agency agreement with the current holder in due course of my alleged obligation.

Please answer the following fifteen questions related to my alleged obligation and the servicing thereof.

1. Who was the original and who were the subsequent funders of any alleged debt related to my property? And please provide me with all information regarding the original certified security for any alleged debt created related to my property, including all information regarding identity of the ownership entities and chain of title, all original and subsequent funders, and all entitlement information, so I can verify the proper servicing.

2. I have questions about your servicing the alleged debt related to my property. Is the accounting complete and accurate? Please provide me with all complete, proper accounting records with interpretation codes and a spreadsheet of all debits and credits related to any alleged debt regarding my property.

3. After creation, was the alleged debt ever sold, and if so then to whom? Include every assignment executed and include by whom the assignment was executed. Was each person authorized to execute an assignment? Who is the current holder in due course of any alleged debt related to my property? Who is

the current physical custodian of any alleged debt related to my property during the servicing period, which began immediately after the alleged debt was created?

4. Were all entities legally compliant? Please provide me with evidence that any and all entities having anything to do with any alleged debt related to my property were and currently are legally compliant in all aspects of operations and actions taken regarding the servicing of this alleged debt.

5. As the servicer and keeper of records related to any alleged debt on my property, were all good-faith disclosures made? Please provide me with copies of all good-faith disclosures made, and a list of all such disclosures that were required with any alleged debt related to my property.

6. Were all Servicers and Sub-servicers legally compliant in all their actions and operations? Please supply me with evidence of such legal compliance.

7. After the alleged debt was created and during the servicing of same, was any alleged debt related to my property part of any Pool? If so, please send me copies of any and all Pool Agreements and or Pooling Service Agreements with identification of any Pass Through Certificates and the names of the Pool Managers and any Deposit Agreements.

8. Related to servicing of the alleged debt in question, was any alleged debt related to my property covered by any Custodial or Master Purchasing Agreements? If so, please supply me with copies of all such agreements.

9. During the servicing of the alleged debt, was any alleged debt related to my property covered by any Trustee Agreements, Beneficiary Agreements, Appointments, and or Substitutions? If so, please send me copies of all such agreements and or appointments.

10. As servicer, is there any agreement with MERS that in any way affects any alleged debt related to my property? If so, please send me copies of any such agreement.

11. As servicer, were there or have there been any checks or electronic transfers made related to any alleged debt regarding my property? If so, please send me front and back copies of any such checks and also copies of any electronic transfers.

12. As servicer, was there any correspondence written by text, email, fax, hard copy, or other means made to me or any other parties related to any alleged debt regarding my property? If so, please send me copies of the all the same.

13. As servicer, were any documents recorded with any county recording system or other record-keeping system related to any alleged debt regarding my property? If so, please send me copies.

14. As servicer, what attorneys' fees, BPO fees, Inspection fees, if any, have been expended related to any alleged debt regarding my property, and have those fees been charged to an alleged account bearing my name, and have they been applied to any alleged outstanding debt balance, and how, if at all, have I benefited from any such alleged attorneys' fees, BPOs, and or Inspections?

15. As servicer, what, if any, business affiliations, or other affiliations exist, or existed, between and/or among any business entities who have taken any action or have asserted any interest, legal or economic or otherwise, related to any alleged debt regarding my property? Please send me a complete list of any such affiliations.

Sincerely yours,

BORROWER NAME [or BORROWER REPRESENTATIVE'S NAME]

Exhibit B
Short-Form Qualified Written Request

Date:
AGENT NAME
CREDITOR NAME
ADDRESS
CITY, STATE, ZIP

REGARDING: QUALIFIED WRITTEN REQUEST
YOUR [BORROWER/DEBTOR] NAME(S)
STREET ADDRESS [of subject property]
CITY, STATE, ZIP
SSN:
Our File No:
Account Number:

Dear Sir or Madam:

Please treat this letter as a "qualified written request" under Section 6(e) of the Real Estate Settlement Procedures Act, 12 U.S.C. 2605(e). This request is made on behalf of my Clients, the above-named debtors, based on the upcoming case about the proper application of payments from the debtors to interest, principal, escrow advances, and expenses (in that order of priority as provided for in the loan instruments); about your use of suspense accounts in connection with debtors' payments; about your use of legacy late charges with respect to mortgage payments; about your use of automatically triggered property inspections and broker price opinion charges and fees based on legacy accounting for arrears; and about legal fees and expenses that have been attached to this account in the form of corporate advances that have neither been applied for nor approved. Specifically, I am requesting the following information:

1. A complete and original life-of-loan transaction history to the date of your response to this letter prepared by the Servicer from its own records using its own system and default servicing personnel. Also, please identify the

mortgage servicing software you use in connection with this loan (MSP, LSAMS, etc).

2. A copy of your Key Loan Transaction history, bankruptcy work form, XLS spreadsheet, or any other manually prepared spreadsheet or record of all accounts associated with this mortgage loan (this includes both recoverable and non-recoverable and restricted and non-restricted accounts).

3. A full and complete, plain-English definitional dictionary of all transaction codes and other similar terms used in the records requested above or any of the other documents or records requested or referred to herein.

4. If this is a MERS or MOM loan, please attach a copy of all MERS Milestone Reports.

5. If this is a MERS or MOM loan, please attach a copy of all MIN Reports.

6. Please identify the full name, address, and telephone number of the current holder of the original mortgage Note, including the name, address, and phone number of any trustee under the trust or other fiduciary. This request is being made pursuant to Section 1641(f)(2) of the Truth in Lending Act, which requires the servicer to identify the holder of the debt.

7. Copies of all collection notes, collection records, communication files, and any other form of recorded data with respect to any communications between you and the debtor.

8. An itemized statement of the full amount needed to reinstate the mortgage as of the date of your response along with an itemized pay-off statement.

9. Copies of all written or recorded communications between you and any non-lawyer third parties regarding this mortgage (including but not limited to LPS Desktop communiqués, NewTrak communications, NewInvoice transmittals, NewImage transmittals, electronic communications by email or otherwise, collection notes, and any other form of written or electronic document related to the servicing of or ownership of this loan).

10. All P-309 screen shots of the history all of the accounts (principal, interest, escrow, late charges, legal fees, property inspection fees, broker price opinion fees, statutory expense fees, miscellaneous fees, corporate advance fees, etc.) associated with this loan.

11. To the extent that the servicer of this mortgage loan has charged the debtor's mortgage loan account any appraisal fees, broker price opinion fees, property inspection/preservation fees, legal fees, bankruptcy/Proof of Claim fees,

recoverable corporate advances, and other fees or costs that were not disclosed to the debtor(s), the debtor(s) dispute(s) any such fees and costs and specifically requests that the account be corrected.

Also be advised that you must acknowledge receipt of this qualified written request within five (5) business days, pursuant to 12 U.S.C. Section 2605(e)(1) (A) as amended effective July 16, 2010, by the Dodd-Frank Financial Reform Act and Reg. X Section 3500.21(e)(1).

You should also be advised that the debtor(s) herein will seek the recovery of damages, costs, and reasonable legal fees for each failure to comply with the questions and requests herein. The debtor(s) also reserve the right to seek statutory damages for each violation of any part of Section 2605 of Title 12 of the United States Code in the amount of $2,000.00 for each violation.

Very truly yours

Attorney for Debtors [sign and print name, date, and notarize]
CC: The Debtors

Exhibit C
Certified Authorization of Borrower

Borrower hereby authorizes its legal counsel to represent its interests regarding matters relating to deeds of trust, mortgages, notes, and loans and other matters related thereto. Failure by Lender to comply with this grant of authority or any reasonable request by the parties acting on my behalf conducting the Loan Review and listed on the Qualified Written Request (QWR) with documented findings of Deceptive Lending Practices may result in immediate legal action and equitable remedies, and may include the demand for rescission, and may include a demand for recovery of costs, and all out of pocket expenses in connection with the review, demand, claim, refund, or damages.

X _____   _____   _____
    Borrower Signature   Social Security Number   Date

Printed Name: _____

X _____   _____   _____
    Borrower Signature   Social Security Number   Date

Printed Name: _____

Notarization: The above signatories produced identification, which is on file with me; a duly authorized Notary Public; and signed the above in my presence.

My Commission Expires: _____ State of: _____

Notary Public: _____ Date: _____

Exhibit D
Mortgage Analysis
Required Documents
Intake Cover Page

Referrer Name: _____

Date Docs Submitted: _____

Referrer Phone Number(s): _____

Subject Property Address for Review: _____

Client Name(s): _____

Client Phone Numbers: _____

Client Current Address: _____

Reviewed by: _____

Date Documents Received: _____

Documents required for all mortgages on each property. Include first, second, and HELOC. Organize separately and use separate cover page for each. Mark (y) if included and (n) if not.

_____1. COPY OF FINAL HUD-1 SETTLEMENT CLOSING STATEMENT

_____2. COPY OF BOTH PRELIMINARY AND FINAL FEDERAL TRUTH-IN-LENDING (TIL)　DISCLOSURES

_____3. COPY OF GOOD-FAITH ESTIMATE (GFE)

_____4. COPY OF 1003 UNIFORM RESIDENTIAL LOAN APPLICATION (ALL PAGES)

_____5. COPY OF APPRAISAL, IF AVAILABLE

_____6. COPY OF NOTE AND MORTGAGE or DEED OF TRUST

_____7. COPY OF ALL CLOSING DOCUMENTS

_____8. COPY OF ANY CORRESPONDENCE RELATED TO CHANGES IN SERVICING AGENT

_____9. COPY OF ANY ASSIGNMENT OF NOTE and/or MORTGAGE

_____10. COPY OF BORROWER'S DRIVERS LICENSE

_____11. COPY OF BORROWER(S) PAGE 2 (AGI) US TAX FORM 1040 FOR 2 YEARS PERIOD PRIOR TO THE CLOSING DATE (THIS IS TO VERIFY INCOME FOR LOAN)

_____12. COPY OF THE MOST RECENT MONTHLY STATEMENT FROM THE CURRENT LOAN SERVICER OR LENDER

_____13. COPY OF ALL DEFAULT OR FORECLOSURE NOTICES AND ANY OTHER CORRESPONDENCE WITH LENDER

_____14. SIGNED COPY OF AGREEMENT EXECUTED BY ALL PARTIES TO THE NOTE, MORTGAGE, OR WITH AN INTEREST IN THE PROPERTY

_____15. SEPARATE CHECK FOR: _____ MADE TO: _____ FOR EACH PROPERTY TO BE CASHED AFTER REVIEW AND ANALYSIS IS COMPLETED

INCLUDE THIS AS A COVER SHEET FOR EACH ANALYSIS REQUESTED!
Please hand deliver, or overnight your own photocopies (not originals).

Exhibit E
Arguments for Temporary Restraining Order and/or Preliminary Injunction

1. Plaintiff has filed a lawsuit complaining that Defendants do not have legal or economic standing to foreclose on Plaintiff's property.

2. Plaintiff does not deny the obligation, but Plaintiff does vigorously deny that any obligation is owed to the Defendants who are only middlemen and not parties of interest.

3. Defendants have "nothing to lose" in this case since Defendants did not loan any money of their own and or have already been fully repaid out of sale proceeds of selling the obligation to other third parties through a securitization scheme devised by investment banks of Wall Street.

4. By contrast, Plaintiff has much to lose be being evicted out of Plaintiff property such as lost equity, both in terms of down payment as well as amortization equity gained over the years of payments, expenses, emotional stress, physical damage and cost of moving, finding new living quarters and expenses related to that, utility deposits, etc.

5. The identity of the true holder in due course of any alleged obligation has not been revealed to the Plaintiff. Defendants are not the true holder in due course.

6. The amount of obligation owing has not been revealed to the Plaintiff since an accounting is required to determine what if any payments have been applied to the obligation in question including payments from cross collateralized payment sources, credit default swaps, insurance funds such as those from AIG, federal bail out funds, T.A.R.P. funds or other sources.

7. Any wrongful eviction upon Plaintiff will be extremely difficult and burdensome to Plaintiff, and will only increase Plaintiff's damages against Defendants when this case is adjudicated on the merits with the assumption that Plaintiff will prevail.

8. Plaintiff has a strong likelihood of success of winning this case on the merits, and therefore requests the court to stay any foreclosure, eviction, unlawful detainer action, and any further negative credit reporting against Plaintiff until this case is heard on the merits and a verdict has been reached.

9. There is no "default" in this case. A default is defined as a payment missed when a payment is owed. There is no payment owed to the Defendants here, hence no default. Neither has Plaintiff received the notices as required by Nevada law for default, acceleration, and notice of sale from a true party of interest to this obligation.

10. Defendants do not have any clear recorded chain of title showing that they have any right or standing to bring a foreclosure action, or eviction action against Plaintiff.

11. Should the true holder in due course appear at a later date and demand satisfaction, Plaintiff will be potentially placed in a precarious position of "Double Financial Jeopardy" if the court allows the current Defendants to wrongfully foreclose or evict Plaintiff from Plaintiff's property.

12. The Court should not allow Defendants' fraudulent actions to continue by enabling defendants to continue their illegal and fraudulent actions. A stay of Defendants actions will allow time for the Courts to determine if Defendants have any legal grounds to proceed. This will protect the rights of the Plaintiff in the meantime.

13. This Temporary Restraining Order involves right to real property and is appropriate to be brought according to the law of this state.

14. According to statutory law, Plaintiff has a right to know the identity of the True Parties who are of interest in Plaintiff's case.

15. The Law also allows for Plaintiff to have Plaintiff's rights clarified to know where plaintiff stands in relation to the claims made by Defendants.

16. Plaintiff should not be required to post any bond because of the likelihood of success by Plaintiff on the merits of the case.

Conversely, it is the Defendants who should be posting a bond since it is the Defendants who by their illegal actions of foreclosure and eviction are attempting to keep Plaintiff from Plaintiff's entitled quiet use of Plaintiff property as shown by the records of Clark County.

Therefore, Borrower respectfully requests the court to grant the Temporary Restraining Order and Preliminary Injunction to enjoin and prevent the Foreclosing Parties from seeking any further action against Borrower and Borrower's property until such time as when Borrower's case is heard and decided on the merits. To do otherwise, only serves to make the Court an unwitting but willing party to Lender's' fraud against Borrower.

Exhibit F
Securitization Overview

"INVESTOR"

WITH CASH TO LOAN $$

CUSTODIAN OF NOTES

TRUSTEE OF MORTGAGE POOL

DEPOSITOR OF NOTES

SPONSOR OF TRUST

SELLER OF NOTES

RATING AGENCIES

INSURING ENTITIES

CREDIT ENHANCEMENTS ENTITIES

AGGREGATOR OF NOTES

ORIGINATORS OF NOTES

MORTGAGE BROKERS IF ANY

NOMINEE BENEFICIARY

"UNWARY BORROWER"

LOOKING TO BORROW MONEY $$

There are only two parties of interest in each transaction, the investor and the borrower. Only the investor and the unwary borrower are parties of interest. All others are middlemen without an interest who only perform a service for a fee and take profit.

Exhibit G
Simple Legal Statements and Questions that Need Answers

1. If the note was securitized, then it was sold, obviously to the purchasers of the securities.

2. Where is the note? Who owns the note? Is it owned by a German Pension Fund, or an Asian Investment Group, or some Hedge Fund? What fractions of the note were included in the thousands of shares of an investment pool sold?

3. If the note was sold, then the seller of the note no longer has an economic or legal interest in the property; i.e., it was sold.

4. Only the true current holder of the note has a legal and economic interest in the property.

5. What is the identity of the true holder of the note?

6. Where is the paper trail and record evidencing that the true holder of the note is just that—the true holder of the note?

7. MERS is only a nominee beneficiary on the deed of trust.

8. MERS takes no loan applications, makes no loans, invests no money, has no economic risk at stake, and is NOT the true holder of the note and has never been a holder of the note. Generally, MERS holds no notes at all.

9. Therefore, MERS has no legal or any economic standing to foreclose on this note or any other note.

10. It would be illegal and fraudulent for the court to allow any party without legal and economic interest to foreclose on the property of another.

11. Since there is no proof of a true holder in due course of the note, there can be neither a foreclosure nor a foreclosure sale because of lack of standing.

12. Therefore, judgment should favor the borrower.

13. Order for quiet title should prevent the foreclosing parties from causing any more issues and problems to the borrower, and remove any illegal liens on borrower's property with damages and costs awarded to the borrower.

Exhibit H
The Established Understanding of Notes and Mortgages/ Deeds of Trust

1. A note is an agreement to repay borrowed money. A note is considered to be a negotiable instrument and is governed by the Uniform Commercial Code (UCC), which has been accepted in all fifty states. Notes are not real property, but are personal property. Notes may be negotiated or sold by endorsement or by a physical transfer and delivery as governed by the UCC. As personal property, Notes are separate legal documents from real property instruments and documents that are used to secure the payment of the loans that are evidenced by the notes. The real property instruments create liens on real property.

2. A Mortgage or a Deed of Trust is a lien on real property. As such it is also an interest in that real property. Mortgages and Deeds of Trust are considered to be security instruments. The lien creates collateral for the money borrowed in a debt. However, the lien does not create the debt itself. Rights created by Mortgages and Deeds of Trust are considered real property rights and are governed by real property law of the jurisdiction where the property is located. UCC law does not govern real property instruments and rights.

3. A note can only be transferred by endorsement, much like endorsing a check. A note cannot be transferred by an assignment. If there is not a space on the note for an endorsement, then an additional document called an allonge can be added to the note. It must be permanently affixed to the note.

4. Mortgage and Deed of Trust rights can only be transferred by an assignment, and they must be recorded in the local records of the county where the property is located.

5. Often a case will arise where the Trustee wants to prove in a court that it owns the loan. One must ask if the Pooling and Servicing Agreement (PSA) of the securitization pool was properly followed in all its regulations for such a transfer to have taken place. This may be determined by looking at the SEC flings of the Edgar system for records of SEC transactions, and also by discovery demands in a law suit. One questions to ask is whether the Note was transferred to the Trustee at the time of securitization? Often the notes were only endorsed in blank and the particular rules were ignored. An assignment in blank is an incomplete real estate document. There should be a clear recorded assignment from A to B, and B to C, and C to D and so on. Often MERS will try to assert

the validity of an assignment from MERS directly to D without a clear unbroken chain of title.

6. Another case can arise when someone want to prove they have standing to foreclose with the rights of a secured creditor under the bankruptcy code. The UCC Sec. 3-301 does allow for an endorsement by (a) a holder or (b) a non-holder in possession who has the rights of a holder. Parties will assert the guidelines of FNMA and FHLMAC, but these are only guides and are not law. There is no assignment without the assignment of either the Mortgage or the Deed of Trust. A holder is not a holder just because they say they are a holder. A Mortgage or a Deed of Trust cannot be enforced without an assignment recorded in the county records. A holder must have some injury from a default. This means that the holder must have some economic interest in the debt. That means that the holder must have loaned some money. It is impossible for a nominee to show an injury since they did not loan any money. There may be glaring inconsistencies of ownership when comparing the records of the Trustee, MERS, the Servicer and FNMA.

Exhibit I
Congressional Written Report Regarding Securitization and Foreclosure of November 18, 2010

Testimony in a New Jersey bankruptcy court case provides proof of the scenario we've depicted, that subprime originators, starting sometime in the 2004-2005 time frame, if not earlier, stopped conveying note (the borrower IOU) to mortgage securitization trust as stipulated in the pooling and servicing agreement. Professor Adam J. Levitin in his testimony before the House Financial Services Committee last week described what the implications would be:

If mortgages were not properly transferred in the securitization process, then mortgage-backed securities would in fact not be backed by any mortgages whatsoever. The chain of title concerns stem from transactions that make assumptions about the resolution of unsettled law. If those legal issues are resolved differently, then there would be a failure of the transfer of mortgages into securitization trusts, which would cloud title to nearly every property in the United States and would create contract rescission/putback liabilities in the trillions of dollars, greatly exceeding the capital of the US's major financial institutions...

Recently, arguments have been raised in foreclosure litigation about whether the notes and mortgages were in fact properly transferred to the securitization trusts. This is a critical issue because the trust has standing to foreclose if, and only if it is the mortgagee. If the notes and mortgages were not transferred to the trust, then the trust lacks standing to foreclose...

If the notes and mortgages were not properly transferred to the trusts, then the mortgage-backed securities that the investors' purchased were in fact non-mortgage-backed securities. In such a case, investors would have a claim for the rescission of the MBS, meaning that the securitization would be unwound, with investors receiving back their original payments at par (possibly with interest at the judgment rate). Rescission would mean that the securitization sponsor would have the notes and mortgages on its books, meaning that the losses on the loans would be the securitization sponsor's, not the MBS investors, and that the securitization sponsor would have to have risk-weighted capital for the mortgages. If this problem exists on a wide-scale, there is not the capital in the financial system to pay for the rescission claims; the rescission claims would be in the trillions of dollars, making the major banking institutions in the United States would be insolvent.

Countrywide, and likely many other subprime originators quit conveying the notes to the securitization trusts sometime in the 2004-2005 time frame. Yet bizarrely, they did not change the pooling and servicing agreements to reflect what appears to be a change in industry practice.

Our evidence of this change was strictly anecdotal; this bankruptcy court filing, posted at StopForeclosureFraud provides the first bit of concrete proof. The key section:

As to the location of the note, Ms. DeMartini testified that to her knowledge, the original note never left the possession of Countrywide, and that the original note appears to have been transferred to Countrywide's foreclosure unit, as evidenced by internal FedEx tracking numbers. She also confirmed that the new allonge had not been attached or otherwise affixed to the note. She testified further that it was customary for Countrywide to maintain possession of the original note and related loan documents.

This is significant for two reasons: first, it points to pattern and practice, and not a mere isolated lapse. Second, Countrywide, the largest subprime originator, reported in SEC filings that it securitized 96% of the loans it originated. So this activity cannot be defended by arguing that Countrywide retained notes because it was not on-selling them; the overwhelming majority of its mortgage notes clearly were intended to go to RMBS trusts, but it appears industry participants came to see it as too much bother to adhere to the commitments in their contracts.

"Whenever we've gotten into situations on the short side, no matter how bad we think it is, it always proven to be worse." The mortgage securitization mess looks to be adhering to this script.

GEORGETOWN UNIVERSITY LAW CENTER
Adam J. Levitin
Associate Professor of Law

Written Testimony of Adam J. Levitin, Associate Professor of Law, Georgetown University Law Center, before the House Financial Services Committee Subcommittee on Housing and Community Opportunity "Robo-Singing, Chain of Title, Loss Mitigation, and Other Issues in Mortgage Servicing"

November 18, 2010, 10:00 am

Witness Background Statement

Adam J. Levitin in an Associate Professor of Law at the Georgetown University Law Center, in Washington, D.C., and Robert Zinman Scholar in Residence at the American Bankruptcy Institute. He also serves as Special Counsel to the Congressional Oversight Panel and has been the Robert Zinman Scholar in Residence at the American Bankruptcy Institute. Before joining the Georgetown faculty, Professor Levitin practiced in the business finance & restructuring department of Weil, Gotshal & Manges, LLP in New York, and served as law clerk to the Honorable Jane R. Roth on the United States Court of Appeals for the Third Circuit.

Professor Levitin holds a J.D. from Harvard Law School, an M.Phil and an A.M. from Columbia University, and an A.B. from Harvard College. Professor Levitin has not received any Federal grants nor has he received any compensation in connection with his testimony. The views expressed in Professor Levitin's testimony are his own and do not represent the positions of the Congressional Oversight Panel.

EXECUTIVE SUMMARY

The US is now in its fourth year of a mortgage crisis in which over 3 million families have lost their homes and another 2.5 million are currently scheduled to lose theirs. Repeated government loan modification or refinancing initiatives have failed miserably. To this sad state of affairs, there now come a variety of additional problems: faulty foreclosures due to irregularities ranging from procedural defects (including, but not limited to robo-signing) to outright counterfeiting of documents; predatory servicing practices that precipitate borrower defaults and then overcharge for foreclosure services that are ultimately paid for by investors; and questions about the validity of transfers in private-label mortgage securitizations. While the extent of these problems is unknown at present, the evidence is mounting that they are not limited to one-off cases, but that there may be pervasive defects throughout the mortgage servicing and securitization processes.

The servicing problems stem from servicers' failed business model. Servicers are primarily in the transaction processing business and are failing miserably at trying to adapt themselves to the loan modification business. Servicers' business model also encourages them to cut costs wherever possible, even if this involves cutting corners on legal requirements, and to lard on junk fees and in-sourced expenses at inflated prices. The financial incentives of mortgage servicers also encourage them to foreclose, rather than modify loans in many cases, even when modification would maximize the net present value of the loan for investors. The chain of title problems are highly technical, but they pose a potential systemic risk to the US economy. If mortgages were not properly transferred in the securitization process, then mortgage-backed securities would in fact not be backed by any mortgages whatsoever. The chain of title concerns stem from transactions that make assumptions about the resolution of unsettled law. If those legal issues are resolved differently, then there would be a failure of the transfer of mortgages into securitization trusts, which would cloud title to nearly every property in the United States and would create contract rescission/putback liabilities in the trillions of dollars, greatly exceeding the capital of the US's major financial institutions. These problems are very serious. At best they present problems of fraud on the court, clouded title to properties coming out of foreclosure, and delay in foreclosures that will increase the shadow housing inventory and drive down home prices. At worst, they represent a systemic risk that would bring the US financial system back to the dark days of the fall of 2008.

Congress would do well to ensure that federal regulators are undertaking a thorough investigation of foreclosure problems and to consider the possibilities for a global settlement of foreclosure problems, loan modifications, and the housing debt overhang on consumers and financial institutions that stagnate the economy and pose potential systemic risk.

TESTIMONY
Madam Chairwoman, Members of the Committee:

Good morning. My name is Adam Levitin. I am an Associate Professor of Law at the Georgetown University Law Center in Washington, D.C., where I teach courses in bankruptcy, commercial law, contracts, and structured finance. I also serve as Special Counsel to the Congressional Oversight Panel for the Troubled Asset Relief Program. The views I express today are my own, however.

We are now well into the fourth year of the foreclosure crisis, and there is no end in sight. Since mid-2007 around eight million homes entered foreclosure,[1] and over three million borrowers lost their homes in foreclosure.[2] As of June 30, 2010, the Mortgage Bankers Association reported that 4.57% of 1-4 family residential mortgage loans (roughly 2.5 million loans) were currently in the foreclosure, process a rate more than quadruple historical averages.

Additionally, 9.85% of mortgages (roughly 5 million loans) were at least a month delinquent.[3]

Percentage of 1-4 Family Residential Mortgages in Foreclosure[4]

Private lenders, industry associations, and two successive administrations have made a variety of efforts to mitigate the crisis and encourage loan modifications and refinancings. A series of much hyped initiatives, such as the FHASecure refinancing program and the Hope4Homeowners have all met what can charitably be described as limited success. FHASecure, predicted to help 240,000 homeowners,[5] assisted only a few thousand borrowers before it wound down,[6] while Hope4 Homeowners, originally predicted to help 400,000 homeowners,[7] had closed only 130 refinancings as of September 30, 2010.[8] The Home Affordable Modification (HAMP) has also failed, producing 495,898 permanent modifications through September 2010. This number is likely to be a high water mark for HAMP, as new permanent modifications are decreasing rapidly while defaults on permanent modifications rise; if current trends continue, by year's end the number of active permanent HAMP modifications will actually decline.

A number of events over the past several months have roiled the mortgage world, raising questions about:

1. Whether there is widespread fraud in the foreclosure process;

2. Securitization chain of title, namely whether the transfer of mortgages in the securitization process was defective, rendering mortgage-backed securities into *non*-mortgagebacked securities;

3. Whether the use of the Mortgage Electronic Registration System (MERS) creates legal defects in either the secured status of a mortgage loan or in mortgage assignments;

4. Whether mortgage servicers' have defaulted on their servicing contracts by charging predatory fees to borrowers that are ultimately paid by investors;

5. Whether investors will be able to "putback" to banks securitized mortgages on the basis of breaches of representations and warranties about the quality of the mortgages.

These issues are seemingly disparate and unconnected, other than that they all involve mortgages. They are, however, connected by two common threads: the necessity of proving standing in order to maintain a foreclosure action and the severe conflicts of interests between mortgage servicers and MBS investors.

It is axiomatic that in order to bring a suit, like a foreclosure action, the plaintiff must have legal standing, meaning it must have a direct interest in the outcome of the litigation. In the case of a mortgage foreclosure, only the mortgagee has such an interest and thus standing. Many of the issues relating to foreclosure fraud by mortgage servicers, ranging from more minor procedural defects up to outright counterfeiting relate to the need to show standing. Thus problems like false affidavits of indebtedness, false lost note affidavits, and false lost summons affidavits, as well as backdated mortgage assignments, and wholly counterfeited notes, mortgages, and assignments all relate to the evidentiary need to show that the entity bringing the foreclosure action has standing to foreclose. Concerns about securitization chain of title also go to the standing question; if the mortgages were not properly transferred in the securitization process (including through the use of MERS to record the mortgages), then the party bringing the foreclosure does not in fact own the mortgage and therefore lacks standing to foreclose. If the mortgage was not properly transferred, there are profound implications too for investors, as the mortgage-backed securities they believed they had purchased would, in fact be non-mortgage-backed securities, which would almost assuredly lead investors to demand that their investment contracts be rescinded, thereby exacerbating the scale of mortgage putback claims.

Putback claims underscore the myriad conflicts of interest between mortgage servicers and investors. Mortgage servicers are responsible for prosecuting on behalf of MBS investors, violations of representations and warranties in securitization deals. Mortgage servicers are loathe to bring such actions, however, not least because they would often be bringing them against their own affiliates. Servicers' failure to honor their contractual duty to protect investors' interest is but one of numerous problems with servicer conflicts of interest, including the levying of junk fees in foreclosures that are ultimately paid by investors and servicing first lien loans while directly owning junior liens.

Many of the problems in the mortgage securitization market (and thus this testimony) are highly technical, but they are extremely serious.[9] At best they present problems of fraud on the court and questionable title to property. At worst, they represent a systemic risk of liabilities in the trillions of dollars, greatly exceeding the capital of the US's major financial institutions.

While understanding the securitization market's problems involves following a good deal of technical issues, it is critical to understand from the get-go that securitization is all about technicalities.

Securitization is the legal apotheosis of form over substance, and if securitization is to work it must adhere to its proper, prescribed form punctiliously. The rules of the game with securitization, as with real property law and secured credit are, and always have been, that dotting "i's" and crossing "t's" matter, in part to ensure the fairness of the system and avoid confusions about conflicting claims to property. Close enough doesn't do it in securitization; if you don't do it right, you cannot ensure that securitized assets are bankruptcy remote and thus you cannot get the ratings and opinion letters necessary for securitization to work. Thus, it is important not to dismiss securitization problems as merely "technical;" these issues are no more technicalities than the borrower's signature on a mortgage. Cutting corners may improve securitization's economic efficiency, but it undermines its legal viability.

Finally, as an initial matter, let me also emphasize that the problems in the securitization world do not affect the whether homeowners owe valid debts or have defaulted on those debts. Those are separate issues about which there is no general controversy, even if debts are disputed in individual cases.[10]

This written testimony proceeds as follows:

Part I presents an overview of the structure of the mortgage market, the role of mortgage servicers, the mortgage contract and foreclosure process.

Part II presents the procedural problems and fraud issues that have emerged in the mortgage market relating to foreclosures.

Part III addresses chain of title issues.

Part IV considers the argument that the problems in foreclosures are mere technicalities being used by deadbeats to delay foreclosure.

Part V concludes.

I. BACKGROUND ON SECURITIZATION, SERVICING, AND THE FORECLOSURE PROCESS

A. MORTGAGE SECURITIZATION

Most residential mortgages in the United States are financed through securitization. Securitization is a financing method involving the issuance of securities against a dedicated cash flow stream, such as mortgage payments, that are isolated from other creditors' claims. Securitization links consumer borrowers with capital market financing, potentially lowering the cost of mortgage capital. It also allows financing institutions to avoid the credit risk, interest rate risk, and liquidity risk associated with holding the mortgages on their own books. Currently, about 60% of all outstanding residential mortgages by dollar amount are securitized.[11] The share of securitized mortgages by number of mortgages outstanding is much higher because the securitization rate is lower for larger "jumbo" mortgages.[12] Credit Suisse estimates that 75% of outstanding first-lien residential mortgages are securitized.[13] In recent years, over 90% of mortgages originated have been securitized.[14] Most second-lien loans, however, are not securitized.[15]

Although mortgage securitization transactions are extremely complex and vary somewhat depending on the type of entity undertaking the securitization, the core of the transaction is relatively simple.[16] First, a financial institution (the "sponsor" or "seller") assembles a pool of mortgage loans. The loans were either made ("originated") by an affiliate of the financial institution or purchased from unaffiliated third-party originators. Second, the pool of loans is sold by the sponsor to a special-purpose subsidiary (the "depositor") that has no other assets or liabilities. This is done to segregate the loans from the sponsor's assets and liabilities.[17]

Third, the depositor sells the loans to a passive, specially created, single-purpose vehicle (SPV), typically a trust in the case of residential mortgages.[18] The SPV issues certificated securities to raise the funds to pay the depositor for the loans. Most of the securities are debt securities—bonds—but there will also be a security representing the rights to the residual value of the trust or the "equity."

Committee, Apr. 13, 2009 "Second Liens and Other Barriers to Principal Reduction as an Effective Foreclosure Mitigation Program" (testimony of Barbara DeSoer, President, Bank of America Home Loans) at 6 (noting that Bank of America owns the second lien mortgage on 15% of the first lien mortgages it services); Hearing Before the House Financial Services Committee, Apr. 13, 2009 "Second Liens and Other Barriers to Principal Reduction as an Effective Foreclosure Mitigation Program" (testimony of David Lowman, CEO for Home Lending, JPMorgan Chase) at 5 (noting that Chase owns the second lien mortgage on around 10% of the first lien mortgages it services). The ownership of the second while servicing the first creates a direct financial conflict between the servicer qua servicer and the servicer qua owner of the second lien mortgage, as the servicer has an incentive to modify the first lien mortgage in order to free up borrower cash flow for payments on the second lien mortgage.

The securities can be sold directly to investors by the SPV or, as is more common, they are issued directly to the depositor as payment for the loans. The depositor then resells the securities, usually through an underwriting affiliate that then places them on the market.

The depositor uses the proceeds of the securities sale (to the underwriter or the market) to pay the sponsor for the loans. Because the certificated securities are collateralized by the residential mortgage loans owned by the trust, they are called residential mortgage-backed securities (RMBS).

A variety of reasons—credit risk (bankruptcy remoteness), off-balance sheet accounting treatment, and pass-through tax status (typically as a REMIC19 or grantor trust)—mandate that the SPV be passive; it is little more than a shell to hold the loans and put them beyond the reach of the creditors of the financial institution.[20]

Loans, however, need to be managed. Bills must be sent out and payments collected. Thus, a third-party must be brought in to manage the loans.[21]

This third party is the servicer. The servicer is supposed to manage the loans for the benefit of the RMBS holders.

Every loan, irrespective of whether it is securitized, has a servicer. Sometimes that servicer is a first-party servicer, such as when a portfolio lender services its own loans. Other times it is a third-party servicer that services loans it does not own. All securitizations involve third-party servicers, but many portfolio loans also have third-party servicers, particularly if they go into default. Third-party servicing contracts for portfolio loans are not publicly available, making it hard to say much about them, including the precise nature of servicing compensation arrangements in these cases or the degree of oversight portfolio lenders exercise over their thirdparty servicers. Thus, it cannot always be assumed that if a loan is not securitized it is being serviced by the financial institution that owns the loan, but if the loan is securitized, it has thirdparty servicing.

Securitization divides the beneficial ownership of the mortgage loan from legal title to the loan and from the management of the loans. The SPV (or more precisely its trustee) holds legal title to the loans, and the trust is the nominal beneficial owner of the loans. The RMBS investors are formally creditors of the trust, not owners of the loans held by the trust.

The economic reality, however, is that the investors are the true beneficial owners. The trust is just a pass-through holding entity, rather than an operating company. Moreover, while the trustee has nominal title to the loans for the trust, it is the third-party servicer that typically exercises legal title in the name of the trustee. The economic realities of securitization do not track with its legal formalities; securitization is the apotheosis of legal form over substance, but punctilious respect for formalities is critical for securitization to work.

Mortgage servicers provide the critical link between mortgage borrowers and the SPV and RMBS investors, and servicing arrangements are an indispensable part of securitization.[22] Mortgage servicing has become particularly important with the growth of the securitization market.

B. THE MORTGAGE SERVICING BUSINESS[24]

The nature of the servicing business in general militates toward economies of scale and automation. Servicing combines three distinct lines of business: transaction processing, default management, and loss mitigation. Transaction processing is a highly automatable business, characterized by large economies of scale. Default management involves collections and activities related to taking defaulted loans through foreclosure. Like transaction processing, default management can be automated,[25] as it does not require any negotiation with the homeowner, insurers, or junior lienholders.[26]

Loss mitigation is considered an *alternative to foreclosure*, and includes activities such as repayment plans, loan modifications, short sales and deeds in lieu of foreclosure. Loss mitigation is always a negotiated process and is therefore labor-intensive and expensive. Not only must the homeowner be agreeable to any loss mitigation solution, but so too must mortgage insurers and junior lienholders if they are parties on the loan. Because each negotiation is separate and requires a trained employee, there are very few opportunities for automation or economies of scale. Labor expenses are also considered overhead, which are all non-reimbursable expenses to servicers. And, to the extent that loss mitigation is in the form of a loan modification, re-default and self-cure risk always lurk in the background. Moreover, loss mitigation must generally be conducted in addition to default management; the servicer must proceed with foreclosure even if attempting to find an alternative, so the cost of loss mitigation is additive. Yet, while taking a loan through foreclosure is likely to involve lower costs than pursuing loss mitigation, it may not ultimately maximize value for RMBS investors because loss severities in foreclosure can easily surpass those on a re-performing restructured loan.

The balance between these different parts of a servicer's business changes over the course of the housing cycle. When the housing market is strong, the transaction processing dominates the servicing business, but when the housing market is weak, default management and loss mitigation become more important.

The very short weighted average life (WAL) of RMBS trusts combined with very low defaults in most economic environments encouraged servicers to place disproportionate weight on performing loan servicing, which historically has been characterized by small servicing fees and enormous economies of scale. Thus, on a typical loan balance of $200,000 today, a servicer might earn between $500 and $1,000 per year.[27] Given the low-level of annual income per loan, the short WAL of each loan, and low default rates in most economic environments before 2006, servicers had few incentives to devote resources to loss mitigation, but large incentives to invest in performing loan automation to capture the large economies of scale. This left servicers wholly unprepared for the elevated level of defaults that began in 2007.

C. RMBS SERVICER COMPENSATION

RMBS servicers' duties and compensation are set forth in a document called a "Pooling and Servicing" agreement (PSA) also governs the rights of the RMBS certificate holders. RMBS servicers are compensated in four ways. First, they receive a "servicing fee," which is a flat fee of 25—50 basis points (bps) and is a first priority payment in the RMBS trust.[28] This is by far the greatest portion of servicer income. This fee is paid out proportionately across all loans regardless of servicer costs through the economic cycle.

Second, servicers earn "float" income. Servicers generally collect mortgage payments at the beginning of the month, but are not required to remit the payments to the trust until the 25th of the month. In the interim, servicers invest the funds they have collected from the mortgagors, and they retain all investment income. Servicers can also obtain float income from escrow balances collected monthly from borrowers to pay taxes and insurance during the course of the year.

Third, servicers are generally permitted to retain all ancillary fees they can collect from mortgagors. This includes things like late fees and fees for balance checks or telephone payments. It also includes fees for expenses involved in handling defaulted mortgages, such as inspecting the property. Finally, servicers can hold securities themselves directly as investors, and often hold the junior-most, residual tranche in the securitization.

Servicers face several costs. In addition to the operational expenses of sending out billing statements, processing payments, maintaining account balances and histories, and restructuring or liquidating defaulted loans, private label RMBS servicers face the expense of "servicing advances."[29] When a loan defaults, the servicer is responsible for advancing the missed payments of principal and interest to the trust as well as paying taxes and insurance on the property. They continue to pay clear through liquidation of the property, unless these advances are not deemed recoverable.

The servicer is able to recover advances it has made either from liquidation proceeds or from collections on other loans in the pool, but the RMBS servicer does not receive interest on its advances. Therefore, advances can be quite costly to servicers in terms of the time value of money and can also place major strains on servicers' liquidity, as the obligation to make advances continues until the loan is liquidated or the servicer believes that it is unlikely to be able to recover the advances. In some cases, servicers have to advance years' worth of mortgage payments to the trust.

While RMBS servicers do not receive interest on servicing advances, they are compensated for their "out-of-pocket" expenses. This includes any expenses spent on preserving the collateral property, including force-placed insurance, legal fees, and other foreclosure-related expenses. Large servicers frequently "in-source" default management expenses to their affiliates.

D. MONITORING OF RMBS SERVICERS

RMBS servicing arrangements present a classic principal-agent problem wherein the agent's incentives are not aligned with the principal and the principal has limited ability to monitor or discipline the agent.

1. Investors

Investors are poorly situated to monitor servicer behavior because they do not have direct dealings with the servicer. RMBS investors lack information about servicer loss mitigation activity. Investors do not have access to detailed servicer expense reports or the ability to examine loss mitigation decisions.

Investors are able to see only the ultimate outcome. This means that investors are limited in their ability to evaluate servicers' performance on an ongoing basis. And even if investors were able to detect unfaithful agents, they have little ability to discipline them short of litigation.

2. Trustees

RMBS feature a trustee, but the name is deceptive. The trustee is not a common law trustee with general fiduciary duties. Instead, it is a limited purpose corporate trustee whose duties depend on whether there has been a default as defined UN the PSA. A failure to pay all tranches their regularly scheduled principal and interest payments is *not* an event of default.

Instead, default relates to the financial condition of the servicer, whether the servicer has made required advances to the trust, whether the servicer has submitted its monthly report, and whether the servicer has failed to meet any of its covenants under the PSA. Generally, before there is an event of default, the trustee has a few specifically assigned ministerial duties and no others.[30] These duties are typically transmitting funds from the trust to the RMBS investors and providing investors performance statements based on figures provided by the servicer. The trustee's pre-default duties do *not* include active monitoring of the servicer.

Trustees are generally entitled to rely on servicers' data reporting, and have little obligation to analyze it.[31] Indeed, as Moody's has noted, trustees lack the ability to verify most data reported by servicers; at best they can ensure that the reported data complies with any applicable covenant ratios:

The trustee is not in a position to verify certain of the numbers reported by the servicer. For example, the amount of delinquent receivables and the amount of receivables charged off in a given month are figures that are taken from the servicer's own computer systems. While these numbers could be verified by an auditor, they are not verifiable by the trustee.[32]

Likewise, as attorney Susan Macaulay has observed, "In most cases, even if the servicer reports are incorrect, or even fraudulent, absent manifest error, the trustee simply has no way of knowing that there is a problem, and must allocate the funds into the appropriate accounts, and make the mandated distributions, in accordance with the servicer reports."[33]

Macaulay further notes that: Similarly, trustees usually wait for servicers to notify them of defaults,[34] and Moody's has noted that trustees are often unresponsive to information from third parties indicating that an unreported default might have occurred.[35] Thus, trustees enforce servicer representations and warranties largely on the honor system of servicer self-reporting.

For private-label securities, trustees also lack the incentive to engage in more vigorous monitoring of servicer loss mitigation decisions. The trustee does not get paid more for more vigorous monitoring. The trustee generally has little ability to discipline the servicer except for litigation. Private-label RMBS trustees have almost no ability to fire or discipline a servicer.

Servicers can only be dismissed for specified acts, and these acts are typically limited to the servicer's insolvency or failure to remit funds to the trust. Occasionally servicers may be dismissed if default levels exceed particular thresholds.

Trustees also have no interest in seeing a servicer dismissed because they often are required to step in as back-up servicer.[36] In the event of a servicer default, the trustee takes over as servicer (which includes the option of subcontracting the duties), and assumes the duty of making servicing advances to the trust. The back-up servicer role is essentially an insurance policy for investors, and activation of that role is equivalent to payment on a claim; a trustee that has to act as a back-up servicer is likely to lose money in the process, especially when some of the trustees do not themselves own servicing operations.

Trustees also often have close relationships with particular servicers. For example, Professor Tara Twomey and I have shown that Bank of America/Countrywide accounts for nearly two-thirds of Deutsche Bank's RMBS trustee business.[37]

In such circumstances, trustees are unlikely to engage in meaningful monitoring and disciplining of servicers.[38] Amherst Securities points out that early payment default provisions are not effectively enforced by trustees, to the point where in cases where borrowers did not make a single payment on the mortgage, only 37 percent were purchased out of the trust, much smaller amounts for loans making only one to six payments.[39] Thus, for private-label RMBS, there is virtually no supervision of servicers.[40] GSE and Ginnie Mae securitization have greater oversight of servicers. The GSEs serve as master servicers on most of their RMBS; they therefore have a greater ability to monitor servicer compliance. The GSEs require servicers to foreclose according to detailed timelines, and servicers that fail to comply face monetary penalties.

It is almost always an event of default under the indenture if the trustee does not receive a servicer rport within a specified period of time, and the trustee must typically report such a failure to the investors, any credit enhancement provider, the rating agencies and others.

However, the trustee generally has no duties beyond that with respect to the contents of the report, although under the TIA, the trustee must review any reports furnished to it to determine whether there is any violation of the terms of the indenture. Presumably this would include verifying that any ratios represented in any reports conform to financial covenants contained in the indenture, etc. It would not however, requirethe trustee to go beyond the face of the report, i.e. to conduct further investigation to determine whether the data underlying the information on the reports presented to it were, in fact, true. Virtually all indentures, whether or not governed by the TIA, explicitly permit the trustee to rely on statements made to the trustee in officers' certificates, opinions of counsel and documents delivered to the trustee in the manner specified within the indenture.

3. Ratings and Reputation

Like any repeat transaction business, servicers are concerned about their reputations. But reputational sanctions have only very weak discipline on servicer behavior.

While Regulation AB requires servicers to disclose information about their experience and practices,[42] they are not required to disclose information about performance of past pools they have serviced. In any event, reputational sanctions are ineffective because loss severities are more likely to be attributed to underwriting quality than to servicing decisions. Rating agencies also produce servicer ratings, but these ratings are a compilation of the evaluation of servicers on a multitude of characteristics. Rating agencies have been known to incorporate features of Freddie Mac's servicer performance profiles in their servicer assessments and to incorporate loss mitigation performance into their ratings. But details of their methodology used to measure these assessments are not disclosed. They give no indication of whether a servicer is likely to make loss mitigation decisions based solely on the interests of the securitization trust. Ratings are also combined with other criteria, such as the servicer's own financial strength and operational capacity. In other words, servicer ratings go to the question of whether a servicer will have to be replaced because it is insolvent or lacks the ability to service the loans, with much less weight given to whether the servicer acts in the investors' interests.

C. THE MORTGAGE CONTRACT AND FORECLOSURE PROCESS

The mortgage contract consists of two documents, a promissory note (the "note" or the "mortgage loan") and a security instrument (the "mortgage" or the "deed of trust").[43] The note is the IOU that contains the borrower's promise to repay the money loaned. If the note is a negotiable instrument, meaning that it complies with the requirements for negotiability in Article 3 of the Uniform Commercial Code,[44] then the *original physical note* is itself the right to payment.[45]

The mortgage is the document that connects the IOU with the house. The mortgage gives the lender a contingent right to the house; it provides that *if* the borrower does not pay according to the terms of the note, then the lender can foreclose and have the property sold *according to the terms of the mortgage and applicable state and federal law*[41] PMI insurers have recently started to embed staff in servicer shops to monitor loss mitigation efforts.

The applicable law governing foreclosures is state law.[46] State real estate law, including foreclosure law, is non-uniform, making it difficult to state what the law is as a generic matter; there is always the possibility that some jurisdictions may deviate from the majority rule. That said, no state requires a borrower's note to be recorded in local land records for the note to be valid, and, as a general matter, state law does not require the mortgage to be recorded either in order for the mortgage to be enforceable against the borrower. Recording of the mortgage is necessary, however, to establish the mortgage's priority relative to the claims of other parties, including other mortgagees, judgment lien creditors and tax and workmen's' liens against the property. The basic rule of priority is first in time, first in right; the first mortgage to be recorded has senior priority. An unrecorded mortgage will thus, generally have junior priority to a subsequently issued, but recorded mortgage. The difference between enforceability and priority is an important one, discussed in more detail below, in the section of this testimony dealing with MERS.

State law on foreclosures is also non-uniform. Roughly, however, states can be divided into two groups: those where foreclosure actions are conducted through the courts ("judicial foreclosure") and those where foreclosure actions are conducted by private sales ("nonjudicial foreclosure"). This division maps, imperfectly, with whether the preferred security instrument is a mortgage or a deed of trust.[47]

Mortgage loans cost more in states that have judicial foreclosure; what this means is that borrowers in judicial foreclosure states are paying more for additional procedural rights and legal protections; those procedural rights are part of the mortgage contract; failure to honor them is a breach of the mortgage contract. Note, that a default on the mortgage note is not a breach of the contract per se; instead it merely triggers the lender's right to foreclose per the applicable procedure.

In a typical judicial foreclosure proceeding, the homeowner receives a notice of default and if that default is not cured within the required period, the mortgagee then files a foreclosure action in court. The action is commenced by the filing of a written complaint that sets forth the mortgagee's allegations that the homeowner owes a debt that is secured by a mortgage and that the homeowner has defaulted on the debt. Rules of civil procedure generally require that legal actions based upon a writing include a copy of the writing as an attachment to the complaint, although there is sometimes an exception for writings that are available in the public records.

While the mortgage is generally filed in the public records, assignments of the mortgage are often not (an issue complicated by MERS, discussed below), and the note is almost never a matter of public record.

It is important to understand that most judicial foreclosures do not function like the sort of judicial proceeding that is dramatized on television, in which all parties to the case appear in court, represented by attorneys and judgment only follows a lengthy trial. Instead, the norm in foreclosure cases is a default judgment. Most borrowers do not appear in court or contest their foreclosures, and not all of those who do are represented by competent counsel, not least because of the difficulties in paying for counsel.

II. PROCEDURAL PROBLEMS AND FRAUD

The first type of problems in the mortgage market are what might generously be termed "procedural defects" or "procedural irregularities." There are numerous such problems that have come to light in foreclosure cases. The extent and distribution of these irregularities is not yet known. No one has compiled a complete typology of procedural defects in foreclosures; there are, to use Donald Rumsfeld's phrase, certainly "known unknowns" and well as "unknown unknowns."

A. AFFIDAVITS FILED WITHOUT PERSONAL KNOWLEDGE (ROBOSIGNING)

Affidavits need to be based on personal knowledge to have any evidentiary effect; absent personal knowledge an affidavit is hearsay and therefore generally inadmissible as evidence. Accordingly, affidavits attest to personal knowledge of the facts alleged therein.

The most common type of affidavit is an attestation about the existence and status of the loan, namely that the homeowner owes a debt, how much is currently owed, and that the homeowner has defaulted on the loan. (Other types of affidavits are discussed in sections II.B. and II.C., *infra*). Such an affidavit is typically sworn out by an employee of a servicer (or sometimes by a law firm working for a servicer). Personal knowledge for such an affidavit would involve, at the very least, examining the payment history for a loan in the servicer's computer system and checking it against the facts alleged in a complaint. The problem with affidavits filed in many foreclosure cases is that the affiant lacks any personal knowledge of the facts alleged whatsoever. Many servicers, including Bank of America, Citibank, JPMorgan Chase, Wells Fargo, and GMAC, employ professional affiants, some of whom appear to have no other duties than to sign affidavits. These employees cannot possibly have personal knowledge of the facts in their affidavits. One GMAC employee, Jeffrey Stephan, stated in a deposition that he signed perhaps 10,000 affidavits in a month, or approximately 1 a minute for a 40-hour work week.[48] For a servicer's employee to ascertain payment histories in a high volume of individual cases is simply impossible.

When a servicer files an affidavit that claims to be based on personal knowledge, but is not in fact based on personal knowledge, the servicer is committing a fraud on the court, and quite possibly perjury. The existence of foreclosures based on fraudulent pleadings raises the question of the validity of foreclosure judgments and therefore title on properties, particularly if they are still in real estate owned (REO).

B. LOST NOTE AFFIDAVITS FOR NOTES THAT ARE NOT LOST

The plaintiff in a foreclosure action is generally required to produce the note as evidence that it has standing to foreclose. Moreover, under the Uniform Commercial Code, if the note is a negotiable instrument, only a holder of the note (or a *subrogee*)—that is a party in possession of the note— may enforce the note, as the note is the reified right to payment.[49]

There is an exception, however, for lost, destroyed, or stolen notes, which permits a party that has lost possession of a note to enforce it.[50] If a plaintiff seeks to enforce a lost note, it is necessary "to prove the terms of the instrument" as well as the "right to enforce the instrument."[51] This proof is typically offered in the form of a lost note affidavit that attests to the prior existence of the note, the terms of the note, and that the note has been lost.

It appears that a surprisingly large number of lost note affidavits are filed in foreclosure cases. In Broward County, Florida alone, over 2000 such affidavits were filed in 2008-2009.[52] Relative to the national population, that translates to roughly 116,000 lost note affidavits nationally over the same period.[53]

There are two problems with the filing of many lost note affidavits. First, is a lack of personal knowledge. Mortgage servicers are rarely in possession of the original note. Instead, the original note is maintained in the fireproof vault of the securitization trustee's document custodian. This means that the servicer lacks personal knowledge about whether a note has or has not been lost.[54] Merely reporting a communication from the document custodian would be hearsay and likely inadmissible as evidence.

The second problem is that the original note is frequently not in fact lost. Instead, it is in the document custodian's vault. Servicers do not want to pay the document custodian a fee (of perhaps $30) to release the original mortgage, and servicers are also wary of entrusting the original note to the law firms they hire. Substitution of counsel is not infrequent on defaulted mortgages, and servicers are worried that the original note will get lost in the paperwork shuffle if there is a change in counsel. When pressed, however, servicers will often produce the original note, months after filing lost note affidavits. The Uniform Commercial Code (UCC) requires that a party seeking to enforce a note be a holder (or subrogee to a holder) or produce evidence that a note has been lost, destroyed, or stolen; the UCC never contemplates an "inconvenience affidavit" that states that it is too much trouble for a servicer to bother obtaining the original note. But that is precisely what many lost note affidavits are effectively claiming.

Thus, many lost note affidavits are doubly defective: they are sworn out by a party that does not and cannot have personal knowledge of the alleged facts and the facts being alleged are often false as the note is not in fact lost, but the servicer simply does not want to bother obtaining it.

C. JUNK FEES

The costs of foreclosure actions are initially incurred by servicers, but servicers recover these fees off the top from foreclosure sale proceeds before MBS investors are paid. This reimbursement structure limits servicers' incentive to rein in costs and actually incentives them to pad the costs of foreclosure. This is done in two ways. First, servicers charge so-called "junk fees" either for unnecessary work or for work that was simply never done. Thus, Professor Kurt Eggert has noted a variety of abusive servicing practices, including "improper foreclosures or attempted foreclosures; imposition of improper fees, especially late fees; forced-placed insurance that is not required or called for; and misuse of escrow funds."[55]

Servicers' ability to retain foreclosure-related fees has even led them to attempt to foreclose on properties when the homeowners are current on the mortgage or without attempting any sort of repayment plan.[56]

Consistently, Professor Katherine Porter has documented that when mortgage creditors file claims in bankruptcy, they generally list amounts owed that are much higher than those scheduled by debtors.[57]

There is also growing evidence of servicers requesting payment for services not performed or for which there was no contractual right to payment. For example, in one particularly egregious case from 2008, Wells Fargo filed a claim in the borrower's bankruptcy case that included the costs of two brokers' price opinions allegedly obtained in September 2005, on a property in Jefferson Parish, Louisiana when the entire Parish was under an evacuation order due to Hurricane Katrina.[58]

Similarly, there is a frequent problem of so-called "sewer summons" issued (or actually not issued) to homeowners in foreclosures. Among the costs of foreclosure actions is serving notice of the foreclosure (a court summons) on the homeowner. There is disturbing evidence that homeowners are being charged for summons that were never issued. These non-delivered summons are known as "sewer summons" after their actual delivery destination.

One way in which these non-existent summons are documented is through the filing of "affidavits of lost summons" by process servers working for the foreclosure attorneys hired by mortgage servicers. A recent article reports that in Duval County, Florida (Jacksonville) the number of affidavits of lost summons has ballooned from 1,031 from 2000-2006 to over 4,000 in the last two years, a suspiciously large increase that corresponds with a sharp uptick in foreclosures.[59]

Because of concerns about illegal fees, the United States Trustee's Office has undertaken several investigations of servicers' false claims in bankruptcy[60] and brought suit against Countrywide,[61] while the Texas Attorney General has sued American Home Mortgage Servicing for illegal debt collection practices.[62]

The other way in which servicers pad the costs of foreclosure is by in-sourcing their expenses to affiliates at above-market rates. For example, Countrywide, the largest RMBS servicer, force places insurance on defaulted properties with its captive insurance affiliate Balboa.[63] Countrywide has been accused of deliberately extending the time to foreclosure in order to increase the insurance premiums paid to its affiliate, all of which are reimbursable by the trust, before the RMBS investors' claims are paid.[64] Similarly, Countrywide in-sources trustee services in deed of trust foreclosures to its subsidiary Recon Trust.[65] Thus, in Countrywide's' 2007 third quarter earnings call, Countrywide's President David Sambol emphasized that increased revenue from in-sourced default management functions could offset losses from mortgage defaults.

Now, we are frequently asked what the impact on our servicing costs and earnings will be from increased delinquencies and loss mitigation efforts, and what happens to costs. And what we point out is, as I will now, is that *increased operating expenses in times like this tend to be fully offset by increases in ancillary income in our servicing operation, greater fee income from items like late charges, and importantly from in-sourced vendor functions* that represent part of our diversification strategy, a counter-cyclical diversification strategy such as our businesses involved in foreclosure trustee and default title services and property inspection services.[66]

In June, 2010, Countrywide settled with the FTC for $108 million on charges that it overcharged delinquent homeowners for default management services. According to the FTC, Countrywide ordered property inspections, lawn mowing, and other services meant to protect the lender's interest in the property . . . but rather than simply hire third-party vendors to perform the services, Countrywide created subsidiaries to hire the vendors. The subsidiaries marked up the price of the services charged by the vendors—often by 100 percent or more—and Countrywide then charged the homeowners the marked-up fees.[67]

Among the accusations brought against Countrywide in a recent investor notice of default filed by the Federal Reserve Bank of New York along with BlackRock and PIMCO, is that Countrywide has been padding expenses via in-sourcing on the 115 trusts covered by the letter.[68]

Countrywide is hardly the only servicer accused of acting in its interests at the expense of investors. Carrington, another major servicer, also owns the residual tranche on many of the deals it services. Amherst Mortgage Securities has shown that Carrington has been much slower than other servicers to liquidate defaulted loans.[69] Delay benefits Carrington both as a servicer and as the residual tranche investor. As a servicer, delay helps Carrington by increasing the number of monthly late fees that it can levy on the loans. These late fees are paid from liquidation proceeds before any of the MBS investors.

As an investor in the residual tranche, Carrington has also been accused of engaging in excessive modifications to both capture late fees and to keep up the excess spread in the deals, as it is paid directly to the residual holders.[70] When loans were mass modified, Carrington benefited as the servicer by capitalizing late fees and advances into the principal balance of the modified loans, which increased the balance on which the servicing fee was calculated.

Carrington also benefited as the residual holder by keeping up excess spread in the deals and delaying delinquency deal triggers that restrict payments to residual holders when delinquencies exceed specified levels. Assuming that the residual tranche would be out of the money upon a timely foreclosure, delay means that Carrington, as the residual holder, receives many more months of additional payments on the MBS it holds than it otherwise would.[71]

It is important to emphasize that junk fees on homeowners ultimately come out of the pocket of MBS investors. If the homeowner lacks sufficient equity in the property to cover the amount owed on the loan, including junk fees, then there is a deficiency from the foreclosure sale. As many mortgages are legally or functionally non-recourse, this means that the deficiency cannot be collected from the homeowner's other assets. Mortgage servicers recover their expenses off the top in foreclosure sales, before MBS investors are paid. Therefore, when a servicer lards on illegal fees in a foreclosure, it is stealing from investors such as pension plans and the US government.

D. COMPLAINTS THAT FAIL TO INCLUDE THE NOTE

Rule of civil procedure generally require that a compliant based on a writing include, as an attachment, a copy of a writing. In a foreclosure action, this means that both the note and the mortgage and any assignments of either must be attached. Beyond the rules of civil procedure requirement, these documents are also necessary as an evidentiary matter to establish that the plaintiff has standing to bring the foreclosure. Some states have exceptions for public records, which may be incorporated by reference, but it is not always clear whether this exception applies in foreclosure actions. If it does, then only the note, which is not a public record, would need to be attached.

Many foreclosure complaints are facially defective and should be dismissed because they fail to attach the note. I have recently examined a small sample of foreclosure cases filed in Allegheny County, Pennsylvania (Pittsburgh and environs) in May 2010. In over 60 percent of those foreclosure filings, the complaint failed to include a copy of the note. Failure to attach the note appears to be routine practice for some of the foreclosure mill law firms, including two that handle all of Bank of America's foreclosures I would urge the Committee to ask Bank of America whether this was an issue it examined in its internal review of its foreclosure practices.

E. COUNTERFEIT AND ALTERED DOCUMENTS AND NOTARY FRAUD

Perhaps the most disturbing problem that has appeared in foreclosure cases is evidence of counterfeit or altered documents and false notarizations. To give some examples, there are cases in which multiple copies of the "true original note" are filed in the same case, with variations in the "true original note;"[72] signatures on note allonges that have clearly been affixed to documents via Photoshop;[73] "blue ink" notarizations that appear in blank ink; counterfeit notary seals;[74] backdated notarizations of documents issued before the notary had his or her commission;[75] and assignments that include the words "bogus assignee for intervening asmts, whose address is XXXXXXXXXXXXXXXXX."[76]

Most worrisome is evidence that these frauds might not be one-off problems, but an integral part of the foreclosure business. A price sheet from a company called DocEx that was affiliated with LPS, one of the largest servicer support firms, lists prices for various servicesincluding the "creation" of notes and mortgages. While I cannot confirm the authenticity of this price sheet or date it, it suggests that document counterfeiting is hardly exceptional in foreclosure cases.

While the fraud in these cases is not always by servicers themselves, but sometimes by servicer support firms or attorneys, its existence should raise serious concerns about the integrity of the foreclosure process. I would urge the Committee to ask the servicer witnesses what steps they have taken to ascertain that they do not have such problems with loans in their servicing portfolios.

G. THE EXTENT OF THE PROBLEM

The critical question for gauging the risk presented by procedural defects is the extent of the defects. While Federal Reserve Chairman Bernanke has announced that federal bank regulators are looking into the issue and will issue a report this month, I do not believe that it is within the ability of federal bank regulators to gauge the extent of procedural defects in foreclosure cases.

To do so would require, at the very least, an extensive sampling of actual foreclosure filings and their examination by appropriately trained personnel. I am unaware of federal bank regulators undertaking an examination of actual foreclosure filings, much less having a sufficient cadre of appropriately trained personnel. Bank examiners lack the experience or training to evaluate legal documents like foreclosure filings. Therefore, any statement put forth by federal regulators on the scope of procedural defects is at best a guess and at worse a parroting of the "nothing to see here folks" line that has come from mortgage servicers.

I would urge the Committee to inquire with federal regulators as to exactly what steps they are taking to examine foreclosure irregularities and how they can be sure that those steps will uncover the extent of the problem. Similarly, I would urge the Committee to ask the servicer witnesses what specific irregularities they examined during their self-imposed moratoria and by what process. It defies credulity that a thorough investigation of all the potential problems in foreclosure paperwork could be completed in a month or two, much less by servicers that have taken so long to do a small number of loan modifications.

III. CHAIN OF TITLE PROBLEMS

A second problem and potentially more serious problem relating to standing to foreclose is the issue of chain of title in mortgage securitizations.[77] As explained above, securitization involves a series of transfers of both the note and the mortgage from originator to sponsor to depositor to trust. This particular chain of transfers is necessary to ensure that the loans are "bankruptcy remote" once they have been placed in the trust, meaning that if any of the upstream transferors were to file for bankruptcy, the bankruptcy estate could not lay claim to the loans in the trust by arguing that the transaction was not a true sale, but actually a secured loan.[78] Bankruptcy remoteness is an essential component of private-label mortgage securitization deals, as investors want to assume the credit risk solely of the mortgages, not of the mortgages' originators or securitization sponsors. Absent bankruptcy remoteness, the economics of mortgage securitization do not work in most cases.

Recently, arguments have been raised in foreclosure litigation about whether the notes and mortgages were in fact properly transferred to the securitization trusts. This is a critical issue because the trust has standing to foreclose if, and only if it is the mortgagee. If the notes and mortgages were not transferred to the trust, then the trust lacks standing to foreclose. There are several different theories about the defects in the transfer process; I do not attempt to do justice to any of them in this testimony.

It can be very difficult to distinguish true sales from secured loans. For example, a sale and repurchase agreement (a repo) is economically identical to a secured loan from the repo buyer to the repo seller, secured by the assets being sold.

While the chain of title issue has arisen first in foreclosure defense cases, it also has profound implications for MBS investors. If the notes and mortgages were not properly transferred to the trusts, then the mortgage-backed securities that the investors' purchased were in fact *non-mortgage-backed securities*. In such a case, investors would have a claim for the rescission of the MBS,[79] meaning that the securitization would be unwound, with investors receiving back their original payments at par (possibly with interest at the judgment rate).

Rescission would mean that the securitization sponsor would have the notes and mortgages on its books, meaning that the losses on the loans would be the securitization sponsor's, not the MBS investors, and that the securitization sponsor would have to have risk-weighted capital for the mortgages. If this problem exists on a wide-scale, there is not the capital in the financial system to pay for the rescission claims; the rescission claims would be in the trillions of dollars, making the major banking institutions in the United States would be insolvent.

The key questions for evaluating chain of title are what method of transferring notes and mortgages is actually supposed to be used in securitization and whether that method is legally sufficient both as a generic matter and as applied in securitization deals. There is a surprising lack of consensus on both counts. Scholars and attorneys cannot agree either on what methods would work generically, much less determine which were used in securitization transactions.

This means there is a great deal of legal uncertainty over these issues. Even among banks' attorneys, different arguments appear in different litigation. For example, one possible method of transfer—a sale under Article 9 of the Uniform Commercial Code—has never, to my knowledge, been made by banks' attorneys in foreclosure litigation when chain of title has been questioned, even though it is one of the two methods that a recent American Securitization Forum (ASF) white paper argues is proper.[80] Even among the banks' lawyers, then, there is lack of consensus on what law governs transfers.

The following section outlines the potential methods of transfer and some of the issues that arise regarding specific methods. It is critical to emphasize that the law is not settled on most of the issues regarding securitization transfers; instead, these issues are just starting to be litigated.

A. TRANSFERS OF NOTES GENERALLY

As a generic matter, a note can be transferred in one of four methods:

1. The note can be sold via a contract of sale, which would be governed by the common law of contracts.

2. If the note is a negotiable instrument,[81] it could be negotiated, meaning that it would be transferred via endorsement and delivery, with the process

governed by Article 3 of the Uniform Commercial Code (UCC).[82] The endorsement can either be a specific endorsement or an endorsement in blank.

3. The note could be converted into an electronic note and transferred according to the provisions of the federal E-SIGN Act.[83]

4. The note could be sold pursuant to UCC Article 9, if it was sold after 2001.[84] In 49 states (South Carolina being the exception), Article 9 provides a method for selling a promissory note, which requires that there be an authenticated (signed) agreement, value given, and that the seller have rights in the property being transferred.[85] This process is very similar to a common law sale.

B. TRANSFERS OF MORTGAGES GENERALLY

There is general agreement that as a generic method, any of these methods of transfer would work to effectuate a transfer of the note. No method is mandatory. Whether or not the chosen process was observed in practice, is another matter, however.[86] Concerns about noncompliance is discussed below.

There are also several conceivable ways to transfer mortgages, but there are serious doubts about the validity of some of the methods:

1. The mortgage could be assigned through the traditional common law process, which would require a document of assignment. There is general consensus that this process works.

2. The mortgage could be negotiated. This method of transfer is of questionable effectiveness. A mortgage is not a negotiable instrument, and concepts of negotiability do not fit well with mortgages. For example, if a mortgage were negotiated in blank, it should become a "bearer mortgage," but this concept is utterly foreign to the law, not least as the thief of a bearer mortgage would have the ability to enforce the mortgage figure out who would be required to grant a release of the mortgage upon payoff. And, in many states (so-called title theory states), a mortgage is considered actual ownership of real property, and real property must have a definite owner (not least for taxation purposes).

3. The mortgage could "follow the note" per common law. While there is a good deal of case law using this mellifluous phrase, common law is not wholly settled on the principle,

4. The mortgage could "follow the note" if it is an Article 9 transfer.[87] There is consensus that this process would work *if* Article 9 governs the transfer of the note.

C. TRANSFERS IN RESIDENTIAL MORTGAGE SECURITIZATION TRANSACTIONS

All the methods described above for transferring notes and mortgages are simply generic methods. There may be additional requirements for a valid transfer, either as a function of trust law or as agreed upon by the parties themselves by contract. Notably, the American Securitization Forum's white paper considers neither of these possibilities.[88]

1. Trust Law

Trust law creates additional requirements for transfers. RMBS typically involve a transfer of the assets to a New York common law trust. Transfers to New York common law trusts are governed by the common law of gifts. In New York, such a transfer requires actual delivery of the transferred assets in a manner such that no one else could possibly claim ownership.[89] This is done to avoid fraudulent transfer concerns. For a transfer to a New York common law trust, the mere recital of a transfer, is insufficient to effectuate a transfer;[90] there must be delivery in as perfect a manner as possible.[91] Similarly, an endorsement in blank might not be sufficient to effectuate a transfer *to a trust* because endorsement in blank turns a note into bearer paper to which others could easily lay claim.

2. Private Contract

The UCC is simply a set of default rules.[92] Parties are free to contract around it, and need not do so explicitly.[93] Parties can thus impose by contract additional requirements for transfers to those in Articles 3 and 9 or, alternatively, ease the requirements. PSAs appear to be precisely this type of variation by agreement from the UCC. If so, then they would govern the transfers as a simple matter of contract law. Deviation from the PSA requirements would be allowed, but only by the extent permitted by contract law, and even if there were a deviation that constituted a material breach of the contract, it would not void the transfer on a self-executing basis.

3. Private Contract + Trust Law

Trust law and private contract law combine to make a much more rigid set of transfer requirements that contract law would by itself. New York law provides that a trustee's authority is limited to that provided in the trust documents.[94] New York law also provides that any transfer in contravention of the trust documents is void.[95] Therefore, if the PSA—the trust document— says that the transfer must be done in a certain way and the transfer did not comply, the transfer is void, irrespective of whether it would comply with the Uniform Commercial Code or other law. The trust document creates a higher level of conduct to which the transfer must comply.

PSAs require a specific form of transfer. First, the PSA contains a recital of the transfer.[96] But per New York trust law, that recital alone is insufficient to effectuate a transfer to a common law trust.[97] Second, PSAs contain a provision that calls for delivery to the trustee for every mortgage loan in the deal of the original mortgage note bearing all intervening endorsements showing a complete chain of endorsement from the originator to the last endorsee, endorsed *"Pay to the order of _____, without recourse"* and signed (which may be by facsimile signature) in the name of the last endorsee by an authorized officer.[98]

The reason for requiring this complete chain of endorsement from originator up through the Depositor before a final endorsement to the trust is to provide a clear evidentiary basis for all of the transfers in the chain of title in order to remove any doubts about the bankruptcy remoteness of the assets transferred to the trust. Absent a complete chain of endorsements, it could be argued that the trust assets were transferred directly from the originator to the trust, raising the concern that if the originator filed for bankruptcy, the trust assets could be pulled back into the originator's bankruptcy estate

D. COMPLIANCE

Regardless of the legal method that applies for transferring notes and mortgages, there is a question of whether there was compliance with that method in actual securitization deals. The American Securitization Forum white paper says nothing on this count, nor can it; evaluating compliance would involve examining actual loan files. This is something that federal bank regulators should be doing, and I would urge the Committee to underscore that point in conversations with the regulators.

There are, of course, a multitude of potential non-compliance problems, including the premature shredding of notes[99] or the signing of assignments by purported agents of now-defunct companies. The scope of these problems is unclear; they may plague individual deals or just individual loans within those deals. On the other hand, if the PSAs set forth the transfer requirements, there may well be widespread non-compliance with the endorsement requirements of the PSAs. Most notes contain only a single endorsement in blank, not "all intervening endorsements showing a complete chain of endorsement from the originator to the last endorsee" before a final endorsement in blank. This would appear to mean that such transfers are void under New York law and that the mortgages were never actually transferred to the trusts issuing the MBS and this could not be corrected because of various timeliness requirements in PSAs.

It bears emphasis that the validity of transfers to the trusts is an unsettled legal issue. It is not as clear as either the American Securitization Forum or any law firm with outstanding securitization opinion letter liability would have one believe. There are questions both about what law actually governs the transfers and about whether there was compliance with the law. If there is a widespread chain of title problem, however, it would create a systemic crisis, as title on most properties in the US would be clouded and the contract rescission/putback liability because of the failed transfers would greatly surpass the market capitalization of the country's major banks.

IV. YES, BUT WHO CARES? THESE ARE ALL DEADBEATS
A. DOES BANKS' CONVENIENCE TRUMP RULE OF LAW?

A common response from banks about the problems in the securitization and foreclosure process is that it doesn't matter as the borrower still owes on the loan and has defaulted. This "No Harm, No Foul" argument is that homeowners being foreclosed on are all a bunch of deadbeats, so who really cares about due process? As JPMorgan Chase's CEO Jamie Dimon put it "for the most part by the time you get to the end of the process we're not evicting people who deserve to stay in their house."[100]

Mr. Dimon's logic condones vigilante foreclosures: so long as the debtor is delinquent, it does not matter who evicts him or how. (And it doesn't matter if there are some innocents who lose their homes in wrongful foreclosures as long as "for the most part" the borrowers are in default.) But that is not how the legal system works. A homeowner who defaults on a mortgage doesn't have a right to stay in the home if the proper mortgagee forecloses, but any old stranger cannot take the law into his own hands and kick a family out of its home. That right is reserved solely for the proven mortgagee.

Irrespective of whether a debt is owed, there are rules about who can collect that debt and how. The rules of real estate transfers and foreclosures have some of the oldest pedigrees of any laws. They are the product of centuries of common law wisdom, balancing equities between borrowers and lenders, ensuring procedural fairness and protecting against fraud. The most basic rule of real estate law is that only the mortgagee may foreclosure.

Evidence and process in foreclosures are not mere technicalities nor are they just symbols of rule of law. They are a paid-for part of the bargain between banks and homeowners. Mortgages in states with judicial foreclosures cost more than mortgages in states without judicial oversight of the foreclosure process.[101] This means that homeowners in judicial foreclosure states are buying procedural protection along with their homes, and the banks are being compensated for it with higher interest rates. Banks and homeowners bargained for legal process, and rule of law, which is the bedrock upon which markets are built function, demands that the deal be honored.

Ultimately the "No Harm, No Foul," argument is a claim that rule of law should yield to banks' convenience. To argue that problems in the foreclosure process are irrelevant because the homeowner owes *someone* a debt is to declare that the banks are above the law.

B. ARE THEY ALL DEADBEATS?

Not every homeowner in foreclosure is a deadbeat. There are some homeowners who are in foreclosure while current on their mortgages, others who are in foreclosure after having been told by their servicers that they have received loan modifications, and others who are in foreclosure because of warehouse lending fraud problems whereby their original lender sold their same mortgage multiple times. There are also homeowners who are in foreclosure because of predatory servicing practices such as charges for forced-placed insurance at way-above-market rates and misapplication of payments (such as illegally applying payments first to late fees and then the principal and interest owed so as to make the payment only qualify as a partial payment, thus incurring another late fee). These homeowners are hardly deadbeats; they are in foreclosure not because of their own behavior, but because of their servicer's behavior.

Ultimately, we don't know how many homeowners in foreclosure are truly in default on their mortgages. To actually determine that would require a detailed examination of homeowners' payment history, an examination that would take several hours in most cases, and homeowners currently lack the right to receive servicing statements showing how their payments are applied

A servicer's assertion that the homeowner is delinquent is not conclusive evidence, especially if the assertion is in a robosigned affidavit. Most homeowners in foreclosure are likely in default, but given that most homeowners lack legal representation, we should be cautious in assuming too much. Sometimes a default judgment is an admission that the plaintiff is correct, and sometimes it is just a sign of lack of resources to litigate.

V. CONCLUSION

The foreclosure process is beset with problems ranging from procedural defects that can be readily cured to outright fraud to the potential failure of the entire private label mortgage securitization system.

In the best case scenario, the problems in the mortgage market are procedural defects and they will be remedied within reasonably quickly (perhaps taking around a year). Remedying them will extend the time that properties are in foreclosure and increase the shadow housing inventory, thereby driving down home prices. The costs of remedying these procedural defects will also likely be passed along to future mortgage borrowers, thereby frustrating attempts to revive the housing market and the economy through easy monetary policy.

In the worst case scenario, there is systemic risk, as there could be a complete failure of loan transfers in private-label securitization deals in recent years, resulting in trillions of dollars of rescission claims against major financial institutions. This would trigger a wholesale financial crisis. Perhaps the most important lesson from 2008 is the need to be ahead of the ball of systemic risk. This means (1) ensuring that federal regulators do a serious investigation as discussed in this testimony above and (2) considering the possible legislative response to a crisis. The sensible course of action here is to avoid gambling on unsettled legal issues that could have systemic consequences. Instead, we should recognize that stabilizing the housing market is the key toward economic recovery, and that it is impossible to fix the housing market unless the number of foreclosures is drastically reduced, thereby reducing the excess inventory that drives down housing prices and begets more foreclosures. Unless we fix the housing market, consumer spending will remain depressed, and as long as consumer spending remains depressed, high unemployment will remain and the US economy will continue in a doldrums that it can ill-afford given the impending demographics of retirement.

This suggests that the best course of action is a global settlement on mortgage issues, the key elements of which must be (1) a triage between homeowners who can and cannot pay with principal reduction and meaningful modifications for homeowners with an ability to pay and speedier foreclosures for those who cannot, (2) a quieting of title on securitized properties, and (3) a restructuring of bank balance sheets in accordance with loss recognition. A critical point in any global settlement, however, must be removing mortgage servicers from the loan modification process. Servicers were historically never in the loan modification business on any scale, and four years of hoping that something would change have demonstrated that servicers never will manage to successfully modify many loans on their own. They lack the capacity, they lack the incentives, and the lack the will.

Endnotes

1   HOPE Now Data Reports.

2   Id.

3   Mortgage Bankers Association, National Delinquency Survey.

4   Mortgage Bankers Association, National Delinquency Surveys.

5   *See, e.g.,* Press Release, US Dep't of Housing and Urban Development, Bush Administration to Help Nearly One-Quarter of a Million Homeowners Refinance, Keep Their Homes; FHA to implement new 'FHASecure' refinancing product (Aug. 31, 2007), *available at* http://www.hud.gov/news/release.cfm?content=pr07-123.cfm; Press Release, US Dep't of Housing and Urban Development, FHA Helps 400,000 Families Find Mortgage Relief; Refinancing on Pace to Help Half-Million Homeowners by Year's End (Oct. 24, 2008), *available at* http://www.hud.gov/news/release.cfm?content=pr08-167.cfm.

6   Michael Corkery, Mortgage 'Cram-Downs' Loom as Foreclosures Mount, WALL ST. J.,, Dec. 31, 2008.

7   Dina ElBoghdady, HUD Chief Calls Aid on Mortgages a Failure, *Washington Post*, Dec. 17, 2008, at A1.

8   *See* FHA Single Family Outlook, Sept. 2010, *at* http://www.hud.gov/offices/hsg/rmra/oe/rpts/ooe/olcurr.xls - 2010-11-02, Row 263 (note that FHA fiscal years begin in October, so that Fiscal Year 2009 began in October 2008). 3

9   I emphasize, however, that this testimony does not purport to be a complete and exhaustive treatment of the issues involved and that many of the legal issues discussed are not settled law, which is itself part of the problem; trillions of dollars of mortgage securitization transactions have been done without a certain legal basis.

10 A notable exception, however, is for cases where the default is caused by a servicer improperly force-placing insurance or misapplying a payment, resulting in an inflated loan balance that triggers a homeowner default.

11   Inside Mortgage Finance, 2010 Mortgage Market Statistical Annual.

12   Id.

13   Ivy L. Zelman et al., *Mortgage Liquidity du Jour: Underestimated No More* 28 exhibit 21 (Credit Suisse, Equity Research Report, Mar. 12, 2007).

14   Inside Mortgage Finance, 2010 Mortgage Market Statistical Annual.

15   Inside Mortgage Finance, 2010 Mortgage Market Statistical Annual. From 2001-2007, only 14% of second lien mortgages originated were securitized. *Id.* Second lien mortgages create a conflict of interest beyond the scope of this paper. In many cases, second lien loans are owned by financial institutions that are servicing (but do not own) the first lien loan. *See* Hearing Before the House Financial Services

16   The structure illustrated is for private-label mortgage-backed securities. Ginnie Mae and GSE securitizations are structured somewhat differently. The private-label structure can, of course, be used to securitize any asset, from oil tankers to credit card debt to song catalogues, not just mortgages.

17   This intermediate entity is not essential to securitization, but since 2002, Statement of Financial Accountings Standards 140 has required this additional step for off-balance-sheet treatment because of the remote possibility that if the originator went bankrupt or into receivership, the securitization would be treated as a secured loan, rather than a sale, and the originator would exercise its equitable right of redemption and reclaim the securitized assets. Deloitte & Touche, *Learning the Norwalk Two-Step*, HEADS UP, Apr. 25, 2001, at 1.

18   The trustee will then typically convey the mortgage notes and security instruments to a "master document custodian," who manages the loan documentation, while the servicer handles the collection of the loans.

19   A REMIC is a real estate mortgage investment conduit, as defined under I.R.C. §§ 860A-860G.

20   *See* Anna Gelpern & Adam J. Levitin, "Rewriting Frankenstein Contracts: Workout Prohibitions in Residential Mortgage Backed Securities," 82 S. CAL. L. REV. 1075, 1093-98. (2009).

21   *See* Kurt Eggert, *Limiting* "Abuse and Opportunism by Mortgage Servicers," 15 Housing Pol'y Debate 753, 754 (2004).

22   The servicing of nonsecuritized loans may also be outsourced. There is little information about this market because it does not involve publicly available contracts and does not show up in standard data.

23   *See* ACE Sec. Corp. Home Equity Loan Trust, Series 2006-NC3, Prospectus Supplement (Form 424B5) S-11 (Nov. 21, 2006), *available at:* http://www.sec.gov/Archives/edgar/data/1380884/000114420406049985/ v058926_424b5.htm.

24   This section of my testimony comes from Adam J. Levitin & Larry Cordell, *What RMBS Servicing Can Learn from CMBS Servicing*, working paper, November 2010.

25 *See In re Taylor,* 407 B.R. 618 (Bankr. E.D. Pa. 2009), *rev'd* 2010 WL 624909 (E.D. Pa. 2010).

26 Arguably servicers have a fourth line of business—the management of real estate owned (REO). REO are foreclosed properties that were not purchased by third-parties at the foreclosure sale. REO management involves caring for and marketing the REO. It does not require negotiations with the homeowner (who is evicted) or junior lienholders (whose liens are generally extinguished by the foreclosure).

27 Servicing fees are generally 25—50 bps, which translates into $500--$1000 per year in servicing fees.

28 Generally the servicing fee is 25 bps for conventional fixed rate mortgages, 37.5 bps for conventional ARM loans, 44 bps for government loans and 50 bps for subprime. *Id.*

29 In Agency securities, servicers generally stop advancing after borrowers owe their fifth payment, at 120 days past due. For GSE loans, they are then removed from the securities and taken on balance sheet. Servicer advances for the four payments are typically not reimbursed until termination.

30 *See, e.g.,* Wells Fargo Mortgage Backed Securities 2006-AR10 Trust § 8.01 ("Prior to the occurrence of an Event of Default of which a Responsible Officer of the Trustee shall have actual knowledge and after the curing of all such Events of Default which may have occurred, the duties and obligations of the Trustee shall be determined solely by the express provisions of this Agreement, the Trustee shall not be liable except for the performance of such duties and obligations as are specifically set forth in this Agreement, no implied covenants or obligations shall be read into this Agreement against the Trustee and, in the absence of bad faith on the part of the Trustee, the Trustee may conclusively rely, as to the truth of the statements and the correctness of the opinions expressed therein, upon any certificates or opinions furnished to the Trustee, and conforming to the requirements of this Agreement."). *See also* Moody's Investor Service, Structured Finance Ratings Methodology: Moody's Re-examines Trustees' Role in ABS and RMBS, Feb. 4, 2003, at 4. (noting "Some trustees have argued that their responsibilities are limited to strictly administrative functions as detailed in the transaction documents and that they have no "fiduciary" duty prior to an event of default.").

31 MBIA Ins. Corp. v. Royal Indem. Co., 519 F. Supp. 2d 455 (2007), *aff'd* 321 Fed. Appx. 146 (3d Cir. 2009) ("Royal argues that Wells Fargo [the trustee] had the contractual obligation to analyze data using certain financial accounting principles and to detect any anomalies that analysis might have uncovered. As Royal suggests, this analysis may not have been very labor-intensive. Yet, the contract did not call for any analysis at all. It simply required Wells Fargo to perform rote comparisons between that data and data contained in various other sources, and to report any numerical inconsistencies. Wells Fargo did just that.").

32 Moody's Investor Service, *supra* note 30, at 4.

33 Susan J. Macaulay, *US: The Role of the Securitisation Trustee,* GLOBAL SECURITISATION AND STRUCTURED FINANCE 2004.

34   Moody's Investor Service, *supra* note 30, at 4.

35   Id.

36   Eric Gross, *Portfolio Management: The Evolution of Backup Servicing*, Portfolio Financial Servicing Company (PFSC) (July 11, 2002) *at:*
      http://www.securitization.net/knowledge/article.asp?id=147&aid=2047.

37   Adam J. Levitin & Tara Twomey, *Mortgage* Servicing, 28 YALE J. ON REG. (forthcoming 2011).

38   *See* Ellington Credit Fund, Ltd. v. Select Portfolio, Inc., No. 1:07-cv-00421-LY, W.D. Tex., Plaintiffs' First Amended Complaint, July 10, 2007 (RMBS residual tranche holder alleging that trustee was aware that servicer was in violation of PSA and failed to act).

39   *See* Amherst Mortgage Insight, "The Elephant in the Room—Conflicts of Interest in Residential Mortgage Securitizations", 15, May 20, 2010.

40   For MBS with separate master and primary servicers, the master servicer may monitor the primary servicer(s), but often the master and primary servicers are the same entity. Recognizing the benefits inherent in effective loss mitigation, Fannie Mae places staff directly in all of the largest servicer shops to work alongside loss mitigation staff at their servicers.

41   Freddie Mac constructed servicer performance profiles to directly monitor servicers, sharing results directly with servicers and rating agencies. Since each GSE insures against credit losses on the loans, their ongoing monitoring provides consistent rules and a single point of contact to approve workout packages and grant exceptions, something absent in private label RMBS.

42   Harry Terris & Kate Berry, *In the Trenches*, AM. BANKER, Aug. 27, 2009. 17 C.F.R. § 229.1108.

43   The note and the mortgage can be combined in a single document, but that is not common practice, both because the mortgage can be granted subsequent to the creation of the debt and because of borrower privacy concerns about the terms of the note, which would become public if the note and mortgage were combined and recorded in local property records.

44   *See* UCC 3-104.

45   UCC 3-203, Cmt. 1 ("An instrument is a reified right to payment. The right is represented by the instrument itself.").

46   There is a federal foreclosure statute that can be utilized by the federal government. *See* 12 U.S.C. §§ 3701-3713 (multi-family property foreclosures); §§3751-3768 (single-family property foreclosures).

47   Mortgages sometimes also include a power of sale, permitting nonjudicial foreclosure. In a deed of trust, the deed to the property is transferred in trust for the noteholder to a deed of trust trustee, often a local attorney. The note remains the property of the lender (the deed of trust beneficiary). When there is a default on the note, the lender notifies the deed

of trust trustee and the lender or its agent is typically appointed as substitute deed of trust trustee to run the foreclosure sale. Most borrowers that the borrower does not contest the foreclosure or appear in court. In most cases, only the lender's attorney appears, and judges routinely dispatch dozens or hundreds of foreclosure cases in a sitting. Homeowners in foreclosure actions are among the most vulnerable of defendants, the least able to insist up on and vindicate their rights, and accordingly the ones most susceptible to abuse of legal process.

48   See Deposition of Jeffrey Stephan, GMAC Mortgage LLC v. Ann M. Neu a/k/a Ann Michelle Perez, No. 50 2008 CA 040805XXXX MB, (15th Judicial Circuit, Florida, Dec. 10, 2009) at 7, *available at*: http://api.ning.com/files/ s4SMwlZXvPu4A7kq7XQUsGW9xEcYtqNMPCm0a2hIS Ju88PoY6ZNqanX7XK41F yf9gV8JIHDme7KcFO2cvHqSEMcplJ8vwnDT/091210g macmortgagevsannmneu1.pdf (stating that Jeffrey Stephan, a GMAC employee, signed approximately 10,000 affidavits a month for foreclosure cases).

49   UCC 3-301; 1-201(b)(21) (defining "holder").

50   UCC 3-309. Note that UCC 3-309 was amended in the 2001 revision of Article 3. The revision made it easier to enforce a lost note. Not every state has adopted the 2001 revisions. Therefore, UCC 3-309 is non-uniform law.

51   UCC 3-309(b).

52   Gretchen Morgenson & Andrew Martin, *Battle Lines Forming in Clash Over Foreclosures*, N.Y. TIMES, Oct. 20, 2010, at A1.

53   According to the US Census Bureau, Broward County's population is approximately 1.76 million, making it .57% of the total US population of 307 million. Broward does have a significantly higher than average foreclosure rate, roughly 12% over the past two years, according to Core Logic Loan Performance data, making it approximately 3 times the national average.

54   The 2001 version of UCC 3-309 permits not only a party that has lost a note but a buyer from such a party to enforce a lost note.

55   Kurt Eggert, *Comment on Michael A. Stegman et al.'s "Preventive Servicing Is Good for Business and Affordable Homeownership Policy": What Prevents Loan Modifications?*, 18 Housing Pol'y Debate 279 (2007).

56   Eggert, *Limiting Abuse, supra* note 21, at 757.

57   Katherine M. Porter, *Mortgage Misbehavior*, 87 TEX. L. REV. 121, 162 (2008).

58   In re Stewart, 391 B.R. 327, 355 (Bankr. E.D. La. 2008).

59   Matt Taibi, "Courts Helping Banks Screw Over Homeowners," *Rolling Stone*, Nov. 25, 2010, at: http://www.rollingstone.com/politics/news/17390/232611?RS_show_page=7.

60   Ashby Jones, *U.S. Trustee Program Playing Tough With Countrywide, Others*, Law Blog (Dec. 3, 2007, 10:01 AM), at: http://blogs.wsj.com/law/2007/12/03/us-trustee-program-playing-tough-with-countrywide-others.

61   Complaint, Walton v. Countrywide Home Loans, Inc. (*In re* Atchely), No. 05-79232 (Bankr. N.D. Ga. filed Feb. 28, 2008).

62   Complaint, State v. Am. Home Mtg. Servicing, Inc., No. 2010-3307 (Tex. Dist. Ct. 448th Jud. Dist. filed Aug. 30, 2010).

63   Amherst Mortgage Insight, 2010, "The Elephant in the Room—Conflicts of Interest in Residential Mortgage Securitizations," 23, May 20, 2010.

64   Id.

65   Center for Responsible Lending, *Unfair and Unsafe: How Countrywide's irresponsible practices have harmed borrowers and shareholders*, CRL Issue Paper, Feb. 7, 2008, at 6–7.

66   Transcript, "Countrywide Financial Corporation Q3 2007 Earnings Call," Oct. 26, 2007 (emphasis added) (also mentioning "Our vertical diversification businesses, some of which I mentioned, are counter-cyclical to credit cycles, like the lender-placed property business in Balboa and like the in-source vendor businesses in our loan administration unit.").

67   FTC, Press Release, June 7, 2010, *Countrywide Will Pay $108 Million for Overcharging Struggling Homeowners; Loan Servicer Inflated Fees, Mishandled Loans of Borrowers in Bankruptcy.*

68   Kathy D. Patrick, Letter to Countrywide Home Loan Servicing LP and the Bank of New York, dated Oct. 18, 2010, *available at*: http://www.scribd.com/Bondholders-Letter-to-BofA-Over-Countrywide-Loans-inc-NY-Fed/d/39686107.

69   Amherst Mortgage Insight, 2010, "The Elephant in the Room—Conflicts of Interest in Residential Mortgage Securitizations", pp. 22–24, May 20, 2010.

70   See Amherst Mortgage Insight, "Why Investors Should Oppose Servicer Safe Harbors", April 28, 2009. Excess spread is the difference between the income of the SPV in a given period and its payment obligations on the MBS in that period, essentially the SPV's periodic profit. Excess spread is accumulated to supplement future shortfalls in the SPV's cash flow, but is either periodically released to the residual tranche holder. Generally, as a further protection for senior MBS holders, excess spread cannot be released if certain triggers occur, like a decline in the amount of excess spread trapped in a period beneath a particular threshold.

71   Carrington would still have to make servicing advances on any delinquent loans if it stretched out the time before foreclosure, but these advances would be reimbursable, and the reimbursement would come from senior MBS holders, rather than from Carrington, if it were out of the money in the residual.

Brief of Antonio Ibanez, Defendant-Appellee, US Bank Nat'l Assn, as Trustee for the Structured Asset Securities Corporation Mortgage Pass-Through Certificates, Series 2006-Z v. Ibanez; Wells Fargo Bank, N.A. as Trustee for ABFC 2005-Opt 1 Trust, ABFC Asset Backed Certificates Series 2005-OPT 1, No 10694, (Mass. Sept. 20, 2010), at 10 (detailing 3 different "certified true copies" of a note allonge and of an assignment of a mortgage); http://4closurefraud.org/2010/04/27/foreclosure-fraud-of-the-week-two-original-wet-ink-notes-submittedinthe-same-case-by-the-florida-default-law-group-and-jpmorgan-chase/ (detailing a foreclosure file with two different "original" wet ink notes for the same loan).

73   http://4closurefraud.org/2010/04/08/foreclosure-fraud-of-the-week-poor-photoshop-skills/.

74   *See* WSTB.com, at http://www.wsbtv.com/video/25764145/index.html.

75   Deposition of Cheryl Samons, Deutsche Bank Nat'l Trust Co., as Trustee for Morgan
     Stanley ABS Capital 1 Inc. Trust 2006-HE4 v.Pierre, No. 50-2008-CA-028558-XXXX-MB
     (15th Judicial Circuit, Florida, May 20, 2009, available at: http://mattweidnerlaw.com/
     blog/wpcontent/uploads/2010/03/depositionsammons.pdf.

76   http://www.nassauclerk.com/clerk/publicrecords/oncoreweb/showdetails.aspx?id=809395
     &rn=0&pi=0&ref=search.

77   Chain of title problems appear to be primarily a problem for private-label securitization,
     not for agency securitization because even if title were not properly transferred for Agency
     securities, it would have little consequence. Investors would not have incurred a loss as the
     result of an ineffective transfer, as their MBS are guaranteed by the GSEs or Ginnie Mae,
     and when a loan in an Agency pool defaults, it is removed from the pool and the owned by
     the GSE or Ginnie Mae, which is then has standing to foreclose.

78   Bankruptcy remote has a second meaning, namely that the trust cannot or will not file
     of bankruptcy. This testimony uses bankruptcy remote solely in the sense of whether the
     trust's assets could be clawed back into a bankruptcy estate via an equity of redemption.
     The Uniform Commercial Code permits a debtor to redeem collateral at face value of the
     debt owed. If a pool of loans bore a now-above-market interest rate, the pool's value could
     be above the face value of the debt owed, making redemption economically attractive.

79   This claim would not be a putback claim necessarily, but could be brought as a general
     contract claim. It could not be brought as a securities law claim under section 11 of the
     Securities Act of 1933 because the statute of limitations for rescission has expired on all
     PLS.

80   American Securitization Forum, *Transfer and Assignment of Residential Mortgage Loans
     in the Secondary Mortgage Market*, ASF white paper series, Nov. 16, 2010, at: http://www.
     americansecuritization.com/uploadedFiles/ASF_White_Paper_11_16_10.pdf. The ASF
     white paper notes that it has been reviewed and approved by 13 major (but unnamed) law
     firms. The ASF white paper does not report whether any of these firms have outstanding
     opinion letter liability on securitization transactions.

81   It is not clear whether mortgage notes are necessarily negotiable instruments.

82   The note endorsement process works just like endorsements on checks and is governed by
     the same law. endorsement to a named endorsee or an endorsement in blank that converts
     the note into bearer paper.

83   15 U.S.C. § 7021. E-SIGN imposes a number of requirements on electronic note transfers
     and also requires consent of the issuer (maker) of the note.

84   The revisions of UCC Articles 1 and 9 went into effect nationally in 2001.

85   UCC 9-203. The language of Article 9 is abstruse, but UCC Revised Article 1 defines
     "security interest" to include the interest of a buyer of a promissory note. UCC 1-201(b)
     (35). Article 9's definition of "debtor" includes a seller of a promissory note, UCC 9-102(a)

(28)(B), and "secured party" includes a buyer of a promissory note, UCC 9-102(a) (72)(D). Therefore UCC 9-203, which would initially appear to address the attachment (enforceability) of a security interest also covers the sale of a promissory note. South Carolina has not adopted the revised Article 1 definition of security interest necessary to make Article 9 apply to sales of promissory notes.

86   Note that common law sales and Article 9 sales do not affect the enforceability of the note against the obligor on the note. UCC 9-308, Cmt.6, Ex. 3 ("Under this Article, attachment and perfection of a security interest in a secured right to payment do not of themselves affect the obligation to pay. For example, if the obligation is evidenced by a negotiable note, then Article 3 dictates the person to whom the maker must pay to discharge the note and any lien security it."). UCC Article 3 negotiation and E-SIGN do affect enforceability as they enable a buyer for value in good faith to be a holder in due course and thereby cut off some of the obligor's defenses that could be raised against the seller. UCC 3-305, 3-306; 15 U.S.C. § 7021(d). and its meaning is not entirely clear (e.g., does it mean that a transfer of the note effectuates a transfer of the mortgage or that the mortgage and the note cannot be separated and both must be transferred—by their own processes— in order for either transfer to work). There are also several instances where the mortgage clearly does not follow the note. For example, the basic concept of a deed of trust is that the security instrument and the note are separated; the deed of trust trustee holds the security, while the beneficiary holds the note. Likewise, the mortgage follows the note concept would imply that the theft of a note also constitutes theft of a mortgage, thereby giving to a thief more than the thief was able to actually steal. Another situation would be where a mortgage is given to a guarantor of a debt. The mortgage would not follow the debt, but would (at best) follow the guarantee. And finally, the use of MERS, a recording utility, as original mortgage (a/k/a MOM) splits the note and the mortgage. MERS has no claim to the note, but MERS is the mortgagee. If taken seriously, MOM means that the mortgage does not follow the note. While MERS might claim that MOM just means that the beneficial interest in the mortgage follows the note, a transfer of the legal title would violate a bankruptcy stay and would constitute a voidable preference if done before bankruptcy.

87   UCC 9-203(g). If the transfer is not an Article 9 transfer, then the Article 9 provision providing that the mortgage follows the note would not apply.

88   *See supra*, note 80.

89   *See* Vincent v. Putnam, 248 N.Y. 76, 83 (N.Y. 1928) ("The delivery must be such as to vest the donee with the control and dominion over the property and to absolutely divest the donor of his dominion and control, and the delivery must be made with the intent to vest the title of the property in the donee....Equity will not help out an incomplete delivery.").

90   *Id.* at 84 ("Mere words never constitute a delivery.").

91   *In re* Van Alstyne, 207 N.Y. 298, 309 (N.Y. 1913).

92   A few provisions of the UCC are mandatory, but these do not affect the chain of title issue.

93   UCC 1-203; 1-201(b)(3) (defining "agreement").

94   14-140 Warren's Weed New York Real Property § 140.58 ("It is a fundamental principle of trust law that the instrument under which the trustee acts is the charter of his rights. Therefore, in administering the trust, he must act in accordance with its terms. This rule

applies to every kind of trustee, regardless of whether the trustee is to hold, invest or pay over income, or to sell or liquidate for the benefit of creditors.").

95   N.Y. E.P.T. L. § 7.2-4.

96   Pooling and Servicing Agreement, Securities Asset Backed Receivables LLC Trust 2005-FR3, § 2.01(b), July 1, 2005, *available at*: http://www.secinfo.com/dRSm6.z1Fa.d.htm ("The Depositor, concurrently with the execution and delivery hereof, hereby sells, transfers, assigns, sets over and otherwise conveys to the Trustee for the benefit of the Certificateholders, without recourse, all the right, title and interest of the Depositor in and to the [mortgage notes].")

97   Vincent v. Putnam, 248 N.Y. 76, 84 (N.Y. 1928) ("Mere words never constitute a delivery.").

98   Pooling and Servicing Agreement, Securities Asset Backed Receivables LLC Trust 2005-FR3, § 2.01(b), July 1, 2005, *available at*: http://www.secinfo.com/dRSm6.z1Fa.d.htm. Deal language may vary, and some PSAs merely require endorsement in blank, not the chain of endorsements on the note. *See, e.g.*, Pooling and Servicing Agreement, Asset Backed Finance Corp. 2006-OPT- 1 Trust, July 1, 2006, *available at* http://www.secinfo.com/dRSm6.v2K1.c.htm#8mq6 (requiring delivery to the trustee of "the original Mortgage Note, endorsed in blank or with respect to any lost Mortgage Note, an original Lost Note Affidavit, together with a copy of the related Mortgage Note" but not of intervening endorsements.)..

99   *See* Florida Bankers' Ass'n Comment to the Florida Supreme Court on the Emergency Rule and Form Proposals of the Supreme Court Task Force on Residential Mortgage Foreclosure Cases, at 4, *at* http://www.scribd.com/doc/38213950/Notes-Are-Destroyed ("The reason many firms file lost note counts as a standard alternative pleading in the complaint' is because the physical document was deliberately eliminated to avoid confusion immediately upon its conversion to an electronic file.").

100 Tamara Keith & Renee Montaigne, *Sorting Out the Banks' Foreclosure Mess,* NPR, Oct. 15, 2010.

101 *See* Karen Pence, Foreclosing on Opportunity: State Laws and Mortgage Credit, 88 REV. ECON. & STAT. 177 (2006) (noting that the availability—and hence the cost—of mortgages in states with judicial foreclosure proceedings is greater than in states with non-judicial foreclosures).

Exhibit J
Client Intake for Bloomberg Securitization Research and Analysis

CLIENT

Name _____

Address_____

City/State/Zip _____

Phones _____

Email_____

Last 4 digits of borrower's Social Security # _____

PROPERTY ADDRESS (if different)

Address_____

City/State/Zip _____

PROPERTY DOCUMENTS (Please scan and send pdf copies of the following):

_____Deed of Trust/Mortgage   _____Communications from attorneys

_____Promissory Note   _____Any recorded assignments of the
                                             Deed of Trust (from Co. Recorder)

_____Latest Loan Statement

_____Notice of Default   _____Substitution of Trustee

_____Notice of Trustee Sale   _____HUD 1 of 1003 Application if
       available

_____Lender Correspondence   _____Other: explain_____

NAMES OF PARTIES on the Note, Deed of Trust/Mortgage

Trust Name _____

APN # _____

Original Lender _____

Address of Lender _____

Original Loan Amount _____

Original Loan Number _____

Lender Loan Servicer _____

Servicer Address _____

NOTICE OF DEFAULT AND NOTICE OF TRUSTEE SALE/FORECLOSURE

Foreclosure Trustee_____

Foreclosure Trustee Address _____

_____

Date of filing of Notice of Default _____

Date of Notice of Trustee Sale_____

Date and Time of Foreclosure Sale _____

Trustee Sale Number _____

I acknowledge that this research and report is not legal advice. I understand that
I need to consult with my own attorney on matters such as this. I understand
that no warranties or guarantees are provided with this information.

Client Signatures _____

_____

Date _____

Resources

Books

The Big Short by Michael Lewis, published by W.W. Norton & Company
> This is an interesting exciting read about Wall Street individuals who were enmeshed in the midst of the securitization trading from the start to the end.

Movies

"Inside Job"
> This movie by Charles Ferguson and narrated by Matt Damon is a professional scathing exposé of the greed and arrogance enacted by Wall Street and our own "government" upon the people of the nation and many others around the world. This is a definite "must see" assignment for your education on this subject.

Websites

www.foreclosuredefensenationwide.com
> This is the website of attorney Jeff Barnes. Jeff posts a number of court orders and other court pleadings.

www.livinglies.wordpress.com
> This is the website of Neil Garfield and Brad Kaiser. Neil and Brad have conducted a number of seminars educating attorneys how to practice foreclosure defense. While a number of attorneys are listed on the "find an Attorney" section, one must be cautioned as to the caliber and approach of these attorneys as all do not actually practice foreclosure defense. Many will only take a fee and attempt a modification with little or no result. Third party vetting is recommended for any referrals from this site.

This website has had well over one million hits and is a plethora of information from articles, court pleadings, court orders, etc. Though not the easiest site to navigate because it is also a blog, nonetheless, there is lots of information. One must be discerning as to the quality of the information.

www.goodgriefamerica.org

> This site is published by Nancie Koerber and Mark Thomas who are located in southern Oregon. While most of the information is focused on the state of Oregon, this site is a good example of how a support group can be established and operated to bring help to many.

www.4closurefraud.org

> This is Carol Asbury's website with lots of general information and assistance regarding foreclosure defense.

www.consumerwarningnetwork.com

> This website was an early pioneer to spread the word that the lender's did not any longer have the note, and was the proponent of the "Produce the Note" approach early in the foreclosure defense actions. The use of videos has been particularly helpful to assist homeowners to get the message.

www.edgar.gov

> This is the official website for the reporting of Security and Exchange commission filings. This site can be helpful in the auditing of the securitization activities of some of the Wall Street securitizers.

www.pacer.gov

> This is the official site of the ederal ankruptcy courts. Many helpful court rulings and orders and pleadings can be found here.

www.mers.com

> This is the website of Mortgage Electronic Registration Systems, Inc. MERS has been named the "Nominee Beneficiary" on millions of deeds of trust and mortgages. Many courts have held that MERS does not have standing to initiate foreclosure.

www.maxgardner.com

O. Max Gardner is the son of a former governor of North Carolina. Max has assisted consumers in the bankruptcy courts for a number of years, and max also teaches a bankruptcy boot camp to train lawyers to use his approach, which is to dispute the mortgage debt in the ankruptcy proceedings.

www.abanet.org/buslaw

This is the site of the American banking Association, and here you will find much helpful information, especially by looking at the articles published in their Business Law publication. This will keep you as up to date as the lenders and banks themselves.

www.stopforeclosurefraud.com

More general information can be found here.

www.jurisdictionary.com?=REFERCOE=CC0008

Recommended whether litigating with an attorney or on your own!

Articles

Google "Christopher Peterson"

Christopher Peterson is a professor of law at the University of Utah law school. Christopher has written numerous articles on the foreclosure debacle since as early as 2007. His writings are scholarly with as much footnoting as text. This is recommended reading for anyone wanting to gain a better understanding of just how the securitization process developed, and the problems with it.

Google "RESPA, TILA, HOEPA, FCRA"

Several federal acts are of interest and intersect directly with the foreclosure subject matter at hand. The Real Estate Settlement Procedures Act (RESPA), the Truth in Lending Act (TILA), the Home Owners Equity Protection Act (HOEPA), and the Fair Credit Reporting Act (FCRA) are all directly related to much of the problems created by the mortgage securitization endeavors.

Google "Securitization Is Illegal"

This is an interesting article that encompasses much of the subject matter showing how the very securitization process is not truly legal as a matter of fact.

Services to Help Solve Your Mortgage Mess Now

Additional copies of this book may be obtained by contacting:
www.SolveMyMortgageMessNow.com

Forensic mortgage audits may be obtained by contacting:
www.SolveMyMortgageMessNow.com

Bloomberg securitization mortgage audits may be obtained by contacting:
www.SolveMyMortgageMessNow.com

Telephonic situation evaluation and support can be obtained by contacting:
www.SolveMyMortgageMessNow.com

Attorney identification, evaluation, and referral can be obtained by contacting:
www.SolveMyMortgageMessNow.com

Full-length DVD videos explaining the mortgage mess and how to solve it can be obtained by contacting: **www.SolveMyMortgageMessNow.com**

Expert witness services can be arranged for by contacting:
www.SolveMyMortgageMessNow.com

For speaking engagements and educational seminars:
www.SolveMyMortgageMessNow.com

Multi-party suits:
www.SolveMyMortgageMessNow.com

Class action lawsuits:
www.SolveMyMortgageMessNow.com

Help Spread the Word!

You can help spread the word and help others solve their mortgage mess by letting them know about this book and the message contained herein. So whether by word of mouth referral, or a gift of this book to someone you care about, or whether through the use of LinkedIn, Twitter, Facebook, Myspace, radio shows, TV shows, emails to friends and associates, we can use the media available to us now to spread the message that help is available. As this movement grows in numbers the extra strength is passed on to everyone. So, please don't be shy about getting out the word about how to solve one's mortgage mess now. Do your best to let others know of this critical and crucial message. The people you help now just may well be the people that will be helping you in some way tomorrow. Thanks for all your efforts, and I will see you later on the journey.

Index

About the Author

Charles Christmas was born in Brownsville, Tennessee, and enjoyed high school athletics winning the state championship in football and in track. College at Abilene Christian University allowed Charles the opportunity to be a national champion in track and field and twice All-American. Charles graduated from the University of Texas School of Law at Austin, and was admitted to the Texas State Bar. After college and law school, Charles spent a year traveling through much of Europe and Asia and spent six months in India. Later, Charles returned to Europe and spent three years in Brussels and three years in London founding urban base communities in each location. After serving in Europe Charles returned to Michigan to become President of TSM Properties, Inc., and developed the world headquarters facilities for Domino's Pizza as well as many commercial real estate projects and properties. Charles has also founded and operated marketing companies and residential real estate brokerage companies. Charles moved to Nevada in 2004 and served as vice president of an agricultural mineral company. For the past three years, Charles has studied the debt reduction industry and has helped numerous homeowners solve their own particular mortgage mess. Charles is a licensed attorney in the state of Texas. Also, Charles is a certified mortgage auditor, certified by the National Association of Mortgage Underwriters. Charles is the father of six children, enjoys composing and performing music, is an avid bicyclist, and enjoys most other outdoor sports as well.

For more information about Charles, or to make comments about this book or this subject matter, please visit: **www.SolveMyMortgageMessNow.com**

Your feedback, comments, and testimonies are very valuable to Charles in his ongoing work of this great cause to help the America homeowner save his home and his way of life. Be sure to look for more books to be available in the near future.

May God bless you!